JOURNALUTION

JOURNALUTION

Journaling to Awaken Your Inner Voice,
Heal Your Life, and Manifest Your Dreams

SANDY GRASON

NEW WORLD LIBRARY
NOVATO, CALIFORNIA

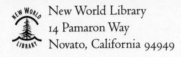 New World Library
14 Pamaron Way
Novato, California 94949

Front cover design by Mary Ann Casler
Text design and typography by Tona Pearce Myers

Library of Congress Cataloging-in-Publication Data
Grason, Sandy.
   Journalution : journaling to awaken your inner voice, heal your life, and manifest your dreams / Sandy Grason.— 1st ed.
      p.   cm.
Includes bibliographical references and index.
ISBN 1-57731-483-2 (pbk. : alk. paper)
1. Self-actualization (Psychology). 2. Diaries—Authorship.
3. Diaries—Therapeutic use. I. Title.
BF637.S4G737 2005
158.1—dc22   2004030825

First printing, May 2005
ISBN 1-57731-483-2
ISBN 13 978-1-57731-483-7

Printed in Canada

g A proud member of the Green Press Initiative

Distributed to the trade by Publishers Group West

10 9 8 7 6 5

This book is lovingly dedicated to my family.

Haley and Emily:
I am so grateful and happy you chose me as your mom.

To my love, Rich:
You somehow saw a possibility in me, long before I could.
I am forever grateful for us. Thank you for always loving me.

Contents

INTRODUCTION
You Say You Want a Journalution —
We All Want to Change Our World   ix

Author's Note   xv

CHAPTER 1
Where Do I Start?   3

CHAPTER 2
The Digging Begins   27

CHAPTER 3
Cleansing and Celebrating the Past   45

CHAPTER 4
Expectations and Major Life Transitions   69

CHAPTER 5

Mirror, Mirror on the Wall   93

CHAPTER 6

Hopes, Dreams, and Visions   117

CHAPTER 7

Conversations with Angels, Elvis, and Beyond   139

CHAPTER 8

Being You   163

Index of Journaling Exercises   179

Journalution Group Guidelines   183

Acknowledgments   189

Notes   193

Share Your Journal with Us   197

About the Author   199

You Say You Want a Journalution — We All Want to Change Our World

Jour·nal·u·tion n 1. *the act of revealing inner wisdom through writing.* 2. *the act of cleansing emotional blocks through writing.* 3. *journal writing to produce or further radical change from within.* 4. *a process for becoming free from confusion or doubt.* 5. *a process for discovering or shining in one's passion and purpose.* 6. *a journey from one place to another (i.e., from where you are now to the life of your dreams).*

Start a journalution. I opened my eyes and heard those words in my head. It was October 14, 2001, 6:00 A.M. *Start a journalution.* I asked my husband if he'd heard of this word *journalution,* but he hadn't. I couldn't find it in the dictionary. I guess I made it up. Or, more accurately, it was given to me.

The word *journalution* sums up the exact feeling I get from journaling. It's so much more than just writing down what's going on in your life. Journalution is a revolution of your soul. It's the inspiration that comes when you release your doubts and fears onto the blank pages of your journal and your inner wisdom comes shining through. It's the ultimate *aha* moment that bubbles up from within.

I've been teaching journaling workshops for many years, and there is still nothing like the feeling I get from seeing someone's eyes light up during a journaling exercise. In one magical moment, a flash of recognition crosses the journaler's face, a whole new world opens up, a life path changes, destiny is revealed, or new possibilities appear where none existed before.

My mission and purpose, which was revealed to me within the pages of my own journals, is to start a global journalution. This means inspiring millions of people to use journaling to heal their lives and manifest their dreams. I know this can happen, because that is exactly what journaling has done for me. It changed who I am. I began journaling when I was twenty-one years old. I was a lost girl searching for answers to life's biggest questions and feeling completely out of touch with my intuition — searching for a spark, a reason to get up in the morning. I poured my heart and soul into the pages of many stacks of journals over the course of more than fifteen years, searching for *me*. I found my true self on the blank page, and you can, too.

I recently attended my twentieth high school reunion. One of my friends brought a large plastic bag full of notes I had written to her in high school. After the festivities, I stayed up until 2:00 A.M. peeking into the life of the sixteen-year-old girl I once was. The high school notes were superficial, mostly about parties and boys. But they brought back memories I had completely forgotten. It reminded me once again how priceless the act of picking up a pen and writing down our thoughts can be. It left me longing to have a deeper conversation with that sixteen-year-old girl. Who was she? What were her dreams? What did she feel when she was alone? I wanted more: more memories, more deep, meaningful conversations, and more glimpses into her soul.

Reading those notes also made me grateful, because I know for sure that when I'm eighty-nine, I will be able to sit down and have many deep and meaningful conversations with the thirty-seven-year-old I am today. I will have captured most of the wonderful, scary, and big moments of my life in journals — as well as lots of little moments, too, which are often the most precious and most easily forgotten.

I am also grateful because I know that my great-great-grandchildren will be able to have those conversations with me, too; they will truly know me through my journals. And, in knowing me, perhaps they will know themselves better.

Your Truth

I don't consider myself to be a journaling guru who is here to tell you everything you need to know about how to keep a journal. But I can tell you that journaling changed my life and who I am more than any other thing I've ever experienced — and I've tried just about everything. I've spent years searching for the answer to my troubles. I am a recovering self-help addict; I've read every book, attended every seminar, and placed a few gurus up on pedestals. I always hoped that the next book or seminar would have the answer for me. The magic pill would be revealed, change my life, and make me happy. Each book and seminar was a step on the journey, and many provided valuable insights that I still hold dear, but they never gave me my answers. Do you know why? Because only I could reveal my answers. I believe that you'll also find this to be true. I am not going to impart some magical wisdom that will immediately grant you true enlightenment, but I will put you in touch with your own magical wisdom.

Every person's truth is different. That is why you will not find your truth in this book or any other book. Your truth is not waiting for you in the next seminar or workshop or guru. But you can begin to find your truth on the blank page. Many great thinkers, artists, and intellectuals keep journals. It is a process of self-discovery unlike any other.

I believe that if you are reading this book, you have been called to add your light and love to the world. A global journalution means a world filled with passionate, abundant, purposeful, joyful, spiritually conscious human beings who will give their gifts and talents back to the planet.

I will show you how to use your journal to find your voice and celebrate your life. I want you to forget your head and lead with your heart. If you want to fully experience this journey, you've got to jump off a few cliffs, reveal yourself completely to another human being, follow the whispers of your soul, and fall deeply in love with your life. Journaling has the power to do all of this by bringing you back into the present moment and turning up the volume of your inner wisdom. I want you to be swept away by the magic of this moment, to float off the page into the heavens. I want you to lose yourself completely in the act of writing. Just when you have fallen under the spell of your creative mind, you will find the key, you will have the revelation, you will feel the *aha!* and a wonderful energy will lift you up. Amazingly, all it takes is a piece of paper and a pen.

You must first be who you really are, then do what you need to do,
in order to have what you want.

— Margaret Young

Author's Note

I've written this book with the intention of inspiring you to use journaling as a tool for healing your life and manifesting your dreams. I have used journaling in this way for many years in my own life. However, I have no professional training as a therapist. While journaling can be useful in resolving personal issues, it is not intended to replace professional advice from a medical doctor or a therapist. My own journaling practice was launched by a suggestion from a psychologist, and I continue to consult with several wonderful coaches; having this professional guidance has made all the difference in my life.

Throughout this book, I have quoted from my own journals as well as those of friends, family members, and workshop participants. The names and identifying characteristics of these individuals have been changed to protect their privacy. Many friends and mentors have kindly granted me permission to use their real names. I am grateful to everyone who shared their experiences with me for use in this book.

JOURNALUTION

CHAPTER 1

Where Do I Start?

What is journaling? In March 1770, John Adams wrote, "The only way to compose myself and collect my thoughts is to set down at my table, place my diary before me, and take my pen into my hand."[1] More recently, Oprah Winfrey was quoted as saying, "Keeping a journal will absolutely change your life in ways you've never imagined."[2] What's the big deal? Why do so many spiritual practices and teachers recommend journaling? As Louise Hay, bestselling author of the book *You Can Heal Your Life*, once wrote, "It is so important for each of us to take that inward journey

and discover what attitudes and beliefs we hold within ourselves."[3]

I believe, as the title of this book suggests, that journaling can be used as a tool for healing and manifesting in your life. Perhaps you have never journaled, and
you want some guidance about how to begin. Or maybe you
have been journaling all your life and you want to go
deeper with your practice. No matter what your past experiences with journaling, this book will meet you where you
are and take you on a transformational journey. I will lead
you through a process that I teach in my journalution
workshops. We'll begin by cleansing the past, forgiving
yourself and others, and getting clear about who you are
and what you want. Then we'll move on to discovering
your passion, developing your life vision, and manifesting
the life you want.

In this first chapter, I will go over some information that
pertains to a new journaler: what you need to get started;
how to choose your own perfect journaling tools; where,
when, how much, and lots of what if's; and my personal
approach to journaling. There are many journaling styles,
and many of you have been journaling for some time; please
always listen to your intuition. If something I am suggesting
doesn't feel right, go with your gut. You know what is best
for you. You are your own best expert.

Everyone has a different motivation for journaling. You
may be dealing with an illness in your family or going
through big changes in your life. You may want to use your
journal for creative purposes, to discover your passion, or to
begin a book of your own. No matter what your intended

purpose, this book will give you a plethora of tools and ideas to make your journaling a fulfilling and rewarding experience.

Why Should I Journal?

The reasons we journal are as varied as the different types of journals piled high on bookstore shelves today. Journaling brings self-knowledge. Writing down your thoughts, venting your emotions about a problem or situation in your life, or just recording scribbles, poetry, inspiring quotations, and dreams brings you closer to who you are. It is a window into what is important to you.

You may have a particular intention for your journal. You may want to leave a legacy for your children or heal from a divorce. You may be working through an illness, or you may need to release emotions in a healthy way. You may be developing material for a novel or otherwise nurturing your creativity.

But you don't need to have a specific reason. A journal can be a companion, a best friend, a way to tap into your intuition, or a place to dump your emotions so they don't land on friends and loved ones. Your journal can be a way to clean out the junk in your head so you can focus on what is really important to you.

Ultimately, writing in a journal is an act of self-love. Your journal is a safe place to get to know yourself and discover who you are. It can bring clarity in a confusing world that bombards us with messages and images of who we *should* be, what we *should* want. A journal allows us to paint a picture of what we want our lives to be, and helps us love ourselves enough to create it. Your writings, musings, and doodles are a way to talk to your soul.

This book will be your guide on the journey into your soul. It may be a healing journey for you, as it was for me, or your journey may have a different purpose. Remain open, and trust that you have all the answers you need inside you. Believe me, you do have those answers, and this book will help you hear them.

Tools of the Trade

The Journal

Selecting a journal is the first step. You can plan a quiet moment for yourself and browse through your favorite bookstore for the journal that calls out to you. Or, in a moment of inspiration, you may grab the nearest spiral notebook, scrap of paper, or blank envelope on which to capture your thoughts. Some people prefer a larger journal because they write big. Some enjoy scribbling in tiny books that fit into their front pockets. Others like to use a huge artist's sketchbook as a canvas. Some people create unusual and beautiful journals by pasting pictures and drawings on the cover and throughout. The company Moleskine makes a legendary pocket journal that boasts a tiny hardbound cover and a hidden interior pocket. It is said that artists have used it for centuries — from Vincent van Gogh to Ernest Hemingway — and it is still sold in bookstores today.

Both lined and unlined journal pages are fully functional. Unlined pages tempt us to draw and doodle amidst the words, but some prefer lined pages because they can't write straight or have enough trouble reading their handwriting without the liberty of a completely blank page. Still others use their computers because they can type really fast; they find that they don't edit themselves as much when typing, and can let their thoughts fly out through their fingertips. For your consistent journaling practice, I encourage you to have something nearby that feels comfortable and works with your lifestyle and personality.

Some people keep separate journals: one for gratitude, one for dreams, and one for everyday matters. Or you might want to keep a travel journal, a nature journal, and a goal journal. Do what feels right for you. I write in only one journal at a time, and I write anything and everything. I like the idea of having a chronological record of everything that is going on in my life — the happy, the sad, the beautiful, and the ugly — all in one place. A workshop participant who was working with her dreams told me that she likes to write down her dreams in a separate journal so that she can recognize patterns that appear. Another woman told me that she keeps separate journals for each of her children, containing messages, advice, and stories about that child's life — a gift for later in their lives.

Dreamy Writing Things

Pens, pencils, markers, and glitter pens. Have you seen the aisle at your local office-supply store lately? The choices are abundant and tremendously personal. Every color of the rainbow is available, in numerous ergonomically designed choices.

Hold a pen or pencil in your fingers, rolling it back and forth against your skin. What does the material feel like? Some are heavy and thin and made of metal, and some are light and round with rubber grippers for your fingers. How does the writing utensil feel as it moves across the paper? Does it glide effortlessly, or scratch against the paper as you form the words? Which do you prefer? Would you like to use an old-fashioned inkpot and feather pen, while visions of Mozart dance in your head? Do you want to use different colored pens or markers to express how you are feeling on a certain day? Do you have visions of doing pencil drawings in the park, using the pencil to shade your subjects in just the right light?

Consider this first decision — selecting your tools — as an exercise in "What do I *really* want? What makes me feel good? What speaks to me?"

There are no wrong answers.

Logistics

Where Should I Journal?

Journal everywhere! Imagine that you are curled up in an overstuffed chair with the warm sunlight streaming through the window just over your right shoulder. Outside, the ocean is dancing with the sunbeams. You hold your journal on your folded legs and pour your thoughts onto the paper. Or perhaps you would prefer a large pine table with a vase of fresh flowers and a beautiful painting that transports you to another land. You write quickly and effortlessly with one hand. The other hand rests on the table, palm down, soaking in the wisdom of the universe, which courses up through your arm and into your heart before it pours onto the blank page. Insights and revelations flow to you, and through you, to share with the world.

Ideally, you would have a cozy corner set aside for writing, surrounded by wonderful things that make you feel safe and loved, bathed in perfect light, and maintained at the perfect temperature. But, truthfully, you can write anywhere, any time. I keep my journal with me, in a canvas bag that contains books I am reading, projects I am working on, and lots of pens and highlighters. I like to know that if I happen to stumble across a poem or quote that moves me, I can jot it down in my journal right then.

If I'm sitting in the doctor's office and two women next to me are having a philosophical discussion that inspires me, I want to be able to begin the same conversation with myself in my journal, right then, while I'm feeling motivated. If I arrive ten minutes early to pick up my daughters at school, I sometimes use those precious moments to capture my life, my feelings, and my identity.

Where would you like to journal?

When Should I Journal?

Is it better to wake up with the sun and journal first thing in the morning, or to reflect on your thoughts and insights

at the end of the day? Does it make a difference if you journal at the same time each day? Some books will tell you that
it's best to write first thing in the morning when your mind
is clear or just after a thirty-minute meditation. Others will
tell you that you should write at the end of the day, capturing all the wonderful things that happened throughout the
day and visualizing what you want to see happen tomorrow.
There are many opinions on these matters, and I believe you
must find what works for you. As you work through this
book, try everything.

I've tried all of the above suggestions, as well as numerous other routines, and I find that different times of day
work for me in different ways. When I am trying to tap into
my creativity, the early morning hours are magical. However,
when I am dealing with a problem, the faster I can get to
my journal and dump all of my emotions, the sooner I will
have my answer. The revelations always come; I just have to
give myself and my problems completely to the blank page.

My journal entries happen at all times of the day and
night. I am often "called" out of bed at three or four o'clock
in the morning, not knowing exactly what I am going to
write. I usually write when I am confused or upset about
something. Journaling is my way of working out problems or
just ranting and raving and getting out the craziness that
sometimes swirls in my head.

Some mothers who keep journals write letters to their
children every year on their birthdays, keeping these books
as future graduation or wedding gifts. Other people journal
after they meditate, recording visions and insights they
received in the process.

Only you will know what feels right to you — and what feels right today could shift as you change and grow. So stay flexible in your journaling practice and let it develop naturally.

When do you see yourself journaling?

How Often Should I Journal?

Some journaling books suggest that you sign a contract with yourself, making a commitment to journal every day for thirty days. This is not one of those books. Why? Because I signed the contracts, made the commitments, and then beat myself up when I missed a day or failed to do it perfectly. I don't want you to go through that.

Most people assume that — because my passion is journaling and I've started a journalution — I must journal every single day, maybe several times a day. Wrong! When I am journaling at three or four o'clock in the morning, it's because I'm working something out. I am confused or upset, or I am very excited about something, and writing about it will let me go back to sleep. Then, days or weeks or even a month might go by before I pick up my journal. Part of the fun is looking at the last few entries to see what was going through my mind during my last session. It's amazing how quickly we forget the details of our lives, how much we obsess over things that will be forgotten in moments.

Think of your journal as a supportive, forgiving friend who is always there for you. Go to your journal for answers or when you need to confide in a friend. Your journal will listen to your problems and help you work them out. You can call on her every day for six months while you are recovering from chemo or after your husband leaves you; she'll be there, ready and eager to listen. Then when you start dating that guy from yoga class, you can ignore her for weeks and she won't get mad. Your journal is there for you when you need it, no matter what. No judgment. No rules. Just write!

Prompts

Prompts are the magic launching pad that will get you writing and quiet your inner critic. A prompt can be anything — a word, a thought, or a phrase — that encourages you to begin journaling. It's an idea, a place to start, or a jumping-off point. If you've never used journaling prompts, you are going to love them. They are completely flexible and endlessly abundant.

In this book, the prompts will be highlighted by the words "Try This." For each prompt, I will give a detailed explanation and visualization. You can also make up your own prompts, using just a word or phrase to launch your journaling. Have a journaling party and ask everyone to write down a prompt and throw it into a bowl; then take turns drawing a prompt and having everyone write from it for ten minutes. (See Journalution Group Guidelines on page 183 for more ideas.)

Ten minutes is only a suggested amount of writing time. Don't feel restricted by it. If you only have five minutes — or even one minute — that's okay, too. For that matter, if you have more than ten minutes, let yourself go; don't stop writing just because the timer went off!

Where Do I Begin?

Many people tell me they would love to keep a journal, but they just don't know how to begin. Relax! You don't have to start at the beginning and tell your life story. The first words in your journal don't have to rival "It was the best of times, it was the worst of times."[4] Just begin where you are.

Here is a description of the first page from one of my journals:

There is a pencil drawing of what I saw while lying in a hammock with my six-year-old daughter. The drawing shows the tree trunk the hammock is tied to, the hammock, my feet wearing woolly socks, my legs from the thighs down, and my journal resting on my legs. I remember that it took me quite a while to draw the hammock; I studied the pattern of the rope, twisting and turning, crissing and crossing. I studied every detail of my socks and the creases in my jeans. I don't think I'm a very good artist, but this picture gives me a big smile. It immediately takes me back to that cool autumn afternoon, our family on vacation in the mountains. My husband was making a fire in the cabin and my daughter and I lazed in the hammock before dinner. What a perfectly wonderful moment, captured forever — better than a photograph to me.

On the facing page is a flower that my daughter drew. Actually, the next four pages have various doodles and drawings, and different forms of "Haley" with flowers attached to the letters. She was so excited to write in *my* journal, rather than hers. And now my journal has captured a six-year-old's doodle drawings, expressing who she was in that moment. Now, only five months later, her signature has changed — just like her smile, as she lost both front teeth last week — but I have that moment, in my journal and in my heart. It has been forever captured by an awkward drawing of a brief, ordinary, yet beautiful moment in time.

You don't have to wait for something big and wonderful to happen in your life in order to start writing. Just begin writing, right now.

Try This
Begin Where You Are

Begin where you are. Date your entries: day of the week, month, year, and time. Describe where you are physically as you begin this journal. Look around and notice your surroundings; write down what you see. How old are you? Married, single, children, job? Give all the specifics. Then describe how you are feeling. How is your life going? What are the things you love about your life right now? What are some things you want to improve or change? Do you have any unresolved emotional issues that you need to explore? Write it all down. Write down a few dreams you have for yourself. Talk about any fears that come to mind. Let yourself write, uncensored, for at least five to ten minutes.

Be Patient and Fearless

I encourage you to be patient with yourself. Words probably won't come pouring out immediately. You aren't likely to find yourself healed and enlightened on the first page. However, you will see a clearer picture of someone coming through to you with each writing session. As if walking toward you out of a fog, this person will come closer and closer and into clearer focus. This someone will guide you; it is your wisdom, your higher self.

Be fearless, or at least bold, as you write. Resist the urge to edit, reword, censor, or scratch out. Just keep your thoughts flowing onto the page, even if they feel jumbled. If your mind keeps jumping from one unrelated thought to another, jump right along with it. You never know; your thoughts may lead you to a magical place. If you are doing a timed writing exercise, the goal is to keep your pen moving. No matter how mixed up or disorganized your thoughts may seem in the process, get them all out onto the paper.

What If I Have Too Much Stuff Inside to Journal?

I was twenty-one years old when I began my first journal. I wrote myself a letter from the perspective of the seven-year-old girl who still lives inside me: *I'm afraid there is something terrible locked inside and if I let even a little bit out, it will all come rushing out like a dam bursting and I won't be able to control it.* Even in that early journal, containing only a handful of entries, my inner wisdom surfaced: *You don't have to control it. You've done a good job of protecting yourself. Now I am here, and I will take care of you. You don't have to be afraid anymore. It's going to be okay.* Your inner wisdom will answer you, too.

You may feel, as I did, that the amount of stuff bottled up inside you is just too overwhelming to express. I promise that you will not die from writing, and you probably won't explode either. The fear of letting it out is normal; you are not alone. Your inner wisdom is buried underneath this fear. Start slowly, and you will begin to experience the relief of letting your emotions pour onto the blank page.

Try This
Interview with Yourself

Now that you've had an opportunity to do some writing, ask yourself these questions in your journal:

- How did journaling feel to you?
- Was it different from what you expected?
- What did you like or dislike about it?
- What came up for you?
- What do you hope will come from your journaling practice?

What If My Writing Isn't Flowing?

It is completely normal if you feel a little uncomfortable at first; everyone feels awkward when they begin. You may hear a critical voice in your head telling you that what you're writing doesn't matter, or that it's not any good. When that voice speaks to you, say "Thank you for sharing," then continue writing. Natalie Goldberg, author of *Writing Down the Bones* and *Wild Mind: Living the Writer's Life*, says: "You are free to write the worst junk in America... or the universe, galaxy, world, hemisphere, Sahara Desert."[5] You may not have aspirations of becoming a published writer, but if you have a critical voice inside, tell it to sit back and pipe down. The magic of journaling comes in allowing yourself to be a channel, and the only way to achieve this state of flow is to stop censoring yourself and let the words pour through you. The editing can come later, if need be.

What If I'm Not a Good Writer?

Remember this new mantra: *I will not judge myself or my journal.* Give yourself permission to write anything, no matter how "good" or "bad" you think it is. If you still hate it in two weeks, you can rip it up and burn it. But give yourself the time and space now to get comfortable. Let your creativity come through. You will discover your voice, and you will begin to enjoy what you've written. You may even want to share some of your journal entries with others.

This process is about self-discovery. It's not about creating a perfectly written product. For now, focus on getting your thoughts and feelings out; don't worry if what you write makes sense or reads well. Just enjoy the experience of journaling, writing whatever pops into your mind.

Try This

Why Do I Want to Journal?

Write "why do I want to journal?" at the top of a blank page in your journal. Set a timer for ten minutes and start writing. Let yourself express all the crazy, wonderful, sad, joyful reasons why you bought this book. What promise or potential called out to you? Write about how you want to feel after you've finished this book. Write the most perfect thing that could come from reading this book. Write down the naggings in your belly that seem to beckon you to journal. Write your most intimate thoughts. What do you believe journaling can do for you? Did something you read or heard make you want to start journaling, or did the inspiration come to you on its own?

Don't overanalyze; just let yourself write whatever pops into your mind. Don't worry if it's messy and jumbled. If the thoughts don't feel like they are flowing the way you think they should, just keep pushing that pen along the paper. Believe that whatever is supposed to come out will come out if you let it. Give yourself the space and the freedom to use up a few pages in your journal with your messy, jumbled thoughts. It's okay.

Draw a picture of something you see. Do you want to be a famous artist? Do you need to get back in touch with your creativity? Do you want to resolve feelings from a troubling relationship? Ask yourself all of these questions and write the first thing that pops into your head. Don't judge it or edit it; just write it down. Your only task is to keep the pen moving for the full ten minutes.

What If Someone Reads My Journal?

Every time I lead a journaling workshop, within the first five minutes a hand will go up tentatively, and the person says, "But I'm afraid that someone will read my journal!" This is a big issue for many people.

Well, I can't promise that it won't happen. My sister backpacked through Europe after college, keeping journals of her adventures. Upon her return home, she accidentally left her journals in the back of a New York City taxicab. She once confided in me that she later wrote, or rather edited her writing, for that stranger — or the boyfriend or roommate who might one day read her intimate thoughts without her permission. But that kind of self-censorship can take all the juice out of journaling. My sister and I came up with a solution for her; try it and see if it helps you, too.

You don't have to let your fear rule your journals. Give yourself two weeks of writing, during which you find a hiding place for your journal, or lock it up, or keep it on your body, or do whatever you need to do to know that your journal is secure for those two weeks. Allow yourself to write anything and everything that is on your mind with the understanding that, at the end of two weeks, you can destroy what you've written if you so desire. See what happens. If you have valid reasons to fear the reactions of a roommate or spouse, you can destroy the journal entries as you go. It is the act of writing down your secret thoughts and dreams that cleanses and empowers you.

The fear of having someone read your private thoughts is usually greater *before* you've actually written them down. Private visions seem scary when they are still floating around in your head, but once you get them down on paper they lose their power over you. They become just another part of you and, as you get to know yourself better, you will begin to accept all sides of your wonderful self. You will become less concerned with what others might think of you, or who might read your journal. Your inner wisdom will resurface and guide you in whatever challenges you may be facing.

My journals contain intimate thoughts, rage-filled rantings, and romantic visions. It is just *me* on the page: good and bad, beautiful and ugly, all of me. When I first began writing these thoughts, I would cover them up with my free hand as I wrote. I was even embarrassed to read them myself. But it didn't take long for me to realize that those embarrassing words were my soul speaking to me, telling me things I didn't think I was ready to hear.

As you grow to know and love all aspects of yourself, you will embrace these "scary," private thoughts and perhaps even want to share them. My intention is to help you get so comfortable and secure in who you are that the fear will dissolve and you will pour your heart and soul onto the page for all to see.

I often use my journal to write letters to my husband or a friend with whom I am having difficulty. Any time I am in need of great communication, I first use my journal to express exactly what's on my mind. Many times I vent in my journal, saying things that I would never say to the person face-to-face. Once the emotion is out, my clarity returns and I can express myself sincerely and without judgment. After I have dumped my thoughts into my journal and gained a greater understanding of the situation, I might even use the journal entry to communicate with that person. For instance, I frequently read my journal to my husband after we have had a disagreement. We find that it brings us closer. And if he happened to read the angry, awful ranting that came before the clarity, my husband would understand that it was only how I was feeling in that moment. It was just a passing emotion. The journal helped me work it out. Now it's over, and we're okay.

Here's a journal entry sent to me from an online journaling group:

> I remember how scary it was for me to write down my private thoughts at first. I would hide my journal under my folded sweaters in the top of my closet, hoping Jim wouldn't find it while I was at work.
>
> But then one day, something happened. I wanted to share it with him. I opened it up and read him a page. My heart pounded. I was revealing things to him that I had never spoken out loud, dreams and desires that embarrassed me. But it felt so good, so liberating.

What If I Don't Have the Time?

Nobody *really* has time to journal, just like nobody *really* has time to exercise. Relax the rules inside your head and simply allow yourself to write when you can. If your journal is with you and you write some of the prompts from this book on the back page, you can do a journaling exercise whenever you have an extra minute or two in the car, in the dentist's waiting room, or even in the bathroom. Let yourself write in short spurts and build from there. There is no perfect way to journal, just as there is no perfect way to meditate or pray. There is only the best way for *you*, and only you can discover that way.

Your journal is for you. Paper and pen will always be there, ready and waiting.

Here is a journal entry from Wendy, age thirty-three, who journals sporadically:

Distractions serve some purpose. They are an escape from the Self. I've allowed myself many distractions lately, and it's been a great vacation, but I'm homesick and my soul needs nourishment. I'm feeling out of control and neglected by myself. I'm ready to be reunited! What was I doing? I'm trying to remember when I lost myself. I stopped doing all of my creative practices. They take time, and others have absorbed my time lately.

I feel the winds of change. Each time I return to myself, I am stronger. When I play guitar a lot and sing a lot and write a lot, I am a happier person, more balanced. Why don't I make time for myself? Where did I go? I give myself away and now there's nothing left to give, so I must replenish the well. Now I will return to myself, return to my journal. It will take me home again.

How Can I Stick with It?

In the past, I purchased journals with the intention of writing in them every day. Then I would abandon them when I accidentally skipped a day or when things got busy. Inevitably, I would find myself standing in another store, clutching yet another beautiful new journal, and thinking, "Maybe this will be *the one*, the journal I will write in every day." I have shelves full of half-empty journals. I used to think of these journals as symbols of disappointment. But now I realize that they don't represent failure; they represent steps on my journey. The journal I started when I was six weeks pregnant took me over three years to complete. It was the first journal I ever "finished," meaning that I wrote on every page. It is tattered and torn. It has stains from spilled snacks and spit-up all over it. That journal was my best friend and savior during a very hazy three years of breastfeeding, colic, clinginess, giggles, and growth for my daughters and me. On the night when I wrote the last entry, I read most of the pages to my husband. It felt as if those three years of our lives were living and breathing on the pages of that journal. I was never more grateful that I had taken the time to write it all down.

I do believe that all of those other journals that sit on my shelves with mostly blank pages are parts of the puzzle that make up my passion for journaling today. I had to keep trying. Those half-empty journals represent the beginnings of my journey, of my mission. They are the first baby steps I took to get where I am today: writing a book to tell you about the wonderful experiences journaling has brought into my life, and encouraging you to begin or continue your own journey.

If you have started journals before and quit, the thing that will make this journal different is how much of *you* goes into it. You can hold back and be safe, only giving little bits and pieces of yourself to the exercises. At the end, you will have a book filled with little parts of yourself, which is still good. Or you can dive in and dig down to the secret parts of yourself, revealing your darkest shadows and uncovering your deepest dreams. You can surrender to the process and welcome whoever wants to show up on the page with you, no matter how frightened or angry or — perhaps even scarier — how wise and magnificent that person may be. This is where your magic lies. How wise and incredible are you willing to be?

Make Your Own Rules

Throw away all the journaling "rules" you've read. There are no rules when it comes to journaling. I am going to give you all kinds of suggestions for different journaling experiences, from flooding the page with your emotions, to seeing the people in your life as mirrors, to using your big life transitions as healing and cleansing opportunities, to having your own conversation with God (or whatever Divine energy you believe in). While some of these suggestions will be distinct exercises, I will also encourage you to discover how flexible the techniques of journaling can be. Use them as you see fit. Listen to your intuition. You are in a process of self-discovery and self-awareness. Figure out what is most useful for you.

This journalution is going to fit with your life and your ways of processing the world. It is not going to be another item to cross off of your to-do list.

I've taken the journey you are embarking on, and I am still traveling and learning and growing. What I've learned so far is that you can never predict what might appear on the blank pages of your journal. Many times you will sit, staring, not knowing where to begin. That is where this book comes in. Once you surrender to your own wisdom, you will be led to your destiny and you will enjoy a glorious ride.

There is a blank book out there somewhere, waiting for your words and holding great possibility. It is a revelation waiting to happen. It is a poem asking to be written. It is unlimited creativity ready to be tapped. It is the idea for your novel ready to be discovered. A journal is a blank canvas, waiting for you to paint the life of your dreams.

Let's begin!

CHAPTER 2

The Digging Begins

Many workshop participants tell me that they come to their journal wanting to experience a revelation, and all they can manage is a few monotonous details about their daily life. They judge the words on the page and question whether they are "doing it right." If you've ever stared at a blank page for hours wondering where to begin, you've come to the right place.

Maybe you've started observing your world and writing down what you do each day. But how do you go from writing around an issue to digging into it and through it? Many of us feel awkward when we begin journaling. Often we are not comfortable with the feelings that arise. Although we hunger for self-knowledge, we are not sure how to achieve it.

What stands between you and the magic of journaling? Do you feel awkward? Does it make you uncomfortable to write down secret thoughts that you don't want anyone else to read? Do you feel blocked? Do you not know where to begin or what to write about? This book is designed to help you overcome any journaling fear or block. In this chapter, we will begin to dig a little deeper with your journal entries. Using the exercises in this chapter, we will determine what areas of your life you want to focus on. Then we'll go into more detail in subsequent chapters. This chapter is a taste of what's to come. If you do these journaling exercises, you will be creating a glorious book filled with wonderful personal thoughts and musings. Your journal will become a window into your soul.

Get Brave

It's time to get brave and dig down deep. It takes a certain amount of bravery to pour your deepest emotions, dreams, and desires onto a blank page. Your deepest self will be documented for all of time. I understand the trepidation you may feel, and I am here to help. You are not alone. Almost everyone feels this way when they first begin to experiment with journaling.

What I can tell you is that if you persevere, the rewards of journaling are gigantic. A peaceful energy will surround you and follow you throughout your day. You will feel more calm and centered when faced with stressful situations. Your newfound freedom will spill over into every aspect of your life. Your creative, artistic side will begin to peek through, even in the most mundane moments. Your inner wisdom will show up in your everyday transactions.

I challenge you to not be satisfied with living an ordinary life. Strive to find your voice. Do not wait. The longer you wait, the less likely you are to find your voice at all. You have an opportunity to experiment in finding your voice with your journal. You can dig and play and express yourself in creative ways. And if you don't like what you write, you can destroy the evidence in the nearest fireplace.

However, be wary of your need to write an "acceptable" journal. We all have a need for acceptance, but tribal thinking is the enemy in your journal. Your goal is to discover *your* beliefs, no matter what others may think. Trust *your* inner wisdom, follow *your* intuition, and listen to *your* heart. Write the longings of your soul, and be willing to go out on a limb to express yourself. Your true voice will show up, and if you let it sing to you, it will get stronger and stronger. It all starts with the willingness to write down anything that comes into your mind.

Here's a journal entry sent to me by a twenty-two-year-old woman who is just beginning to dig a little deeper in her journal:

What is it about my life? Sometimes I feel so small. I know it's about something bigger. Bigger than me and you, bigger than everything I'm feeling right now.

Moments grace me and I tap into the power; other moments flash by — unnoticed. I'm sitting in the longing and despair. I float around in a fog of depression and anxiety. Nothing seems to lift me up. Is it up to me? Do I hold the key? The ultimate power, is it within me?

As she allows herself to ask these big questions, you can see that there is wisdom behind her words. In the rhythmic way she expresses her pain, it feels as if she is on the verge of an answer, if only she will keep writing.

Many times, as you are doing the timed writing exercises, it will feel as if nothing is happening. Then, all of a sudden, a breakthrough occurs. If you had stopped at eight minutes, you never would have gotten that great new idea or experienced the revelation. So no matter how awkward it feels, or how much your mind is jumping around, just keep the pen moving for the full ten minutes, or however long you have agreed to write.

The timer triggers an urgent, creative response. Your subconscious mind knows that you have a limited amount of time in which to accomplish a goal or get an answer, and it will respond to this pressure if you give it a chance. The more you practice this subconscious timed writing, the more in the flow you will feel when you journal.

Try This
I Remember

I first discovered this prompt in a writing group as we worked with one of Natalie Goldberg's books. Write the words "I remember" at the top of a blank page in your journal, and set a timer for ten minutes. This gives your brain just enough to get it going so that you can relax and fill in the blanks. Don't worry if it feels as if your mind is jumping from one memory to the next. It doesn't have to flow onto the page as a complete story. This exercise is just for you to feel the act of writing without thinking, without editing, and without judging. If you feel stuck and don't know what to write next, write "I don't remember" and begin again. The point of this exercise is just to let your mind relax and see what happens. Your subconscious will guide you if you let it. Where does it want to take you?

———————————

Helen is fifty-three years old; she's been married thirty-two years and has three children. Here is her journal entry, written in response to the prompt "I remember":

I remember my wedding day. It was so beautiful. I felt like a fairy princess. Isn't that how it's supposed to be? I remember when my son was born; it changed who I was. I remember the "me" who existed before I was a wife and mother. Those roles took over my life until there was nothing left of me. I remember having big dreams of going to law school and changing the world. I saw myself standing on the steps of the White House, defeating the big, bad corporations. Now my husband works for one. The corporation pays our mortgage. We are owned by them. When did I give up my values? Was it one big decision, or the sum of many small compromises? Was it wrong to think that getting married was the best possible next step? Was I crazy to think that I could hang on

to the idealistic young woman and still be a wife and mother? I
remember when my life did not feel so complicated. I only had to
think of what I wanted, and even that seemed like a huge under-
taking at the time. I scoff at how much drama I created back then.
Ah, to be young again, with my whole life ahead of me. Would I
do things differently? They say, "If I knew then what I know
now..." What then? This is definitely something to consider; what
would I change if I had my life to live over again?

This entry triggered another question for Helen to
explore next time she sits down with her journal. She can
continue to write by asking the question, "What would I
change if I had my life to live over again?" It takes her deeper.

What would you change if you had your life to live over
again?

There are often clues hidden in our childhood memories. When we come into the world, we feel the vitality of
life coursing through our bodies. We are connected to the
magic of the world, and every day feels fresh and new. What
are some of the dreams and goals you had when you were a
child? Here's a good exercise to help you remember what
brought you joy when you were a child.

Try This

You... Only Younger

Visualize yourself at the age of seven. See your bedroom,
your house, your yard. Now imagine that you are sitting across
from that little person right now, and you are laughing,

talking, sharing, playing, and having the time of your life. What makes your seven-year-old self happiest? What brings her joy? Write about all the things you loved to do when you were seven years old. Tell me what you loved as a child. How many of these things could you incorporate into your life today? Have fun with this exercise.

Anne was twenty-seven years old and newly married when she wrote this. She told me that she had a difficult time remembering pleasant things from her childhood at first, having grown up with an alcoholic father, but finally something surfaced in this journal entry:

> It is a challenging task to sort through my childhood and find good memories. With so many unpleasant recollections springing to mind, it's easy to reconnect with that scared little girl I used to be. I said a little prayer: "Flood me with good childhood memories, help me reunite with the happy little girl I see in the pictures," and I walked away from my journal for two days.
>
> In the meantime, my husband and I went to the beach. He entertained himself for a few hours playing volleyball while I parked myself near the shore. The smell of salt and the wet breeze blowing my newspaper around reminded me of something I haven't thought about in years: my family loved going to the beach. My parents would pack us all up and trek out to the beach every weekend. I remember now that it was the highlight of my week. My brother and I would create the grandest, most intricate sand castles any seven-year-old has ever seen. I can still feel myself lying beside my sand castle, obliviously covered in wet sand.

*For that short moment, we would feel like a real, normal
family, and that is what brought me the most joy. I don't have to
struggle to find moments and glimpses of normalcy anymore. I
am thankful that I don't have to make an effort to incorporate
that feeling into my life, because it's already there. And I do love
to reminisce about how it feels to lie in the sand and giggle.*

Break Out

The scary thoughts are the ones you need to commit to
paper right away. The writing that makes you nervous or
sends a shiver up your spine is what will take you to a magical place. You can start slowly. Use the prompts in this
book and follow them along. If there is a specific topic you
want to focus on, skip to that chapter and work with those
prompts right away. The sooner you begin writing down the
inner thoughts that are nagging at you, the sooner your
mind and heart will feel clear to lead you to the next step.

There is no wrong way to do this. Just follow your intuition and jump right in.

Marilyn is in her late forties; she gave me this journal
entry after a very brave writing session:

*I don't want to write about my marriage. I can't. It's easier to
pretend that everything is okay. But I know it's not. There's a
place deep down inside of me that refuses to be quiet. It's a whisper that taunts me almost every day: "Your marriage is falling
apart. It hasn't been a real marriage for many years. How long
will you go on like this? Can you resign yourself to a life without*

*love?" I convince myself that everyone feels this way. My friends
are unhappy in their marriages, too. But that doesn't make it any
easier. I can fill my life with luncheons and cocktail parties, and
the kids still keep me very busy. But how much longer will that
last? Soon they will be out on their own — driving, friends,
parties — and living their own lives. What will we do then,
when there is nothing left to talk about? How long will we be
able to exist in a silent marriage, not talking about what really
matters, drifting farther and farther apart — once lovers, now
strangers in a strange place?*

Thoreau once said, "The mass of men lead lives of quiet
desperation and go to the grave with the song still in them."[1]
I meet so many people in my workshops who are feeling just
that: despair. Their lives are not fulfilling. Somewhere along
the way, they went off track. Maybe it was in an attempt to
please a parent or to earn a living, but their lives have become
an endless treadmill of going through the motions, doing
whatever it takes to make it to the next day, only to wake up
and do it all over again. How do you break out of this? Your
journal is a great place to start. When you are willing to
examine the details of your life, you can change them. This
doesn't mean that you should walk out on your husband and
children and run away with the pool boy; it just means that
you can look a little more closely at your dreams and wishes,
and consider what would add vitality to your life.

Determining what issues or fears you may be hiding
from and what brings you the most joy will automatically
lift some of the veil that keeps you in a fog. Don't be
resigned to a life of quiet desperation. Break free. You can

explore what freedom means to you in the pages of your journal.

If you're ready to dive deep into what's really going on with your subconscious, try this next writing exercise.

Try This

I Don't Want to Write About...

Do you really want to dig deep in your journal? Set a timer for ten minutes and write "I don't want to write about..." at the top of a blank journal page. Then go. You may feel a little twinge in your stomach, or a voice may yell, "No! No! Don't write that!" You must be fearless, or at least pretend to be, for the next ten minutes. If you are really having a hard time with this, tell yourself that you can always rip it up after you've finished. Asking yourself again and again, "What do I not want to write about?" will take you deeper and deeper into your fears. Don't forget to ask for guidance as you jump into these deeper questions and allow the voice of wisdom to show up on the page. Alternate between "I don't want to write about..." and "What can I do about..." and let the rest flow through you onto the pages of your journal. Keep writing until the timer goes off!

How did that feel? Did anything surprising show up on the page? Are you holding anything back? Is there something you simply could not allow yourself to write? If this is the case, then you absolutely *must* write it down, right now.

Set the timer again, write this unthinkable thing on a piece
of scrap paper, and when the timer goes off, reread it and
then rip it into a million shreds. The act of writing will
release your answer. The energy it takes to hold onto this
secret fear could be blocking you from your deepest desires.
Writing and releasing these fears onto the paper will open
you up and give your inner wisdom a chance to shine.

If you feel that you were still holding back on this exercise, go back and try it again. Keep trying until you've written down every scary thought that's living inside your mind.
At this point, it doesn't matter if you rip up the journal
entries or keep them; just get them out of your head and
onto the paper.

Using these prompts to break out of your normal rou-
tine should refocus you on what is important to you. As you
get more and more comfortable with releasing your deepest
thoughts and desires, your life will take on new meaning.
Your journal will guide you into a meaningful life.

Surprises on the Blank Page

Dennis, a fifty-five-year-old man who has been journaling for
over thirty years, wrote to me, "I can say that I write in order
to know what I think and feel. I am often surprised by what
comes out."

Being surprised by what shows up in your journal can
happen the very first time you do a writing exercise. Robert,
a man in his mid-forties who had never kept a journal,
attended one of my workshops and felt a huge shift after just
one ten-minute timed writing exercise. I led the participants

through a visualization, then had them write for ten minutes with the prompt "Conversation with Your Ninety-Nine-Year-Old Self" (which follows). In this exercise, participants asked questions of this older, wiser version of themselves.

After the workshop, Robert said to me, "I think something inside me shifted tonight." He confided that, after four heart attacks and two bouts with cancer, he had never allowed himself to imagine that he might live to the age of ninety-nine years, much less be healthy. He told me that the visualization and the journaling allowed him to see a different perspective. It gave him a chance to map out a new path for his life, starting today.

That is one of the surprises that will come from journaling. In a moment, your life can change. You can have a major shift, or an answer may appear. It all depends on how wise you let yourself be.

Try This

Conversation with Your Ninety-Nine-Year-Old Self

Take a deep breath and close your eyes. Imagine yourself at the ripe old age of ninety-nine. You are in perfect health. Maybe you are sitting in a rocking chair on the front porch of your home or working in the garden or walking along a beach or hiking on a nature trail. Your eyes sparkle with the wisdom of life experience. The lines around your eyes and mouth light up when you smile, and you smile often. Breathe in the essence of this wise old soul that inhabits your body; feel its presence within you.

Now go to your journal and have a conversation with this wise, wonderful person. Ask, "What would you have me know? What should I concentrate on in the coming days and years? What things could I do or experience that would have the most positive impact on my life?" Ask all of the hard questions about your current situation and just let the answers flow onto the page. You will probably feel the answers forming in your mind before you have even finished writing the question. Your only job is to allow the answer to appear on the page. Don't edit yourself; let whatever thoughts come into your mind flow into your journal, no matter how silly they may seem to your logical mind. Remember, there are no rules; just write!

Choose Where to Begin

I've given you a few prompts to point you in several directions. Think about what area of your life you would like to focus on in your journal. Are there any particular problems you are struggling with today? What keeps you up at night? What are your first thoughts upon waking up in the morning? These are the whispers of your soul, trying to get through to you. If you are constantly worrying and wondering what's going to happen tomorrow, you are wasting valuable energy on things you *don't* want. That energy could be focused toward creating a life you *do* want.

Each chapter in this book will focus on a particular area of journaling. You can work through them in order, or you may jump straight to the one that calls out to you.

Do you have some unresolved relationship issues, or memories from your past that need forgiveness or letting go? Do you find yourself easily overwhelmed by your life? Do you have angry or stress-induced outbursts on a regular basis? Do you overreact or feel highly emotional? Going back through your life and journaling about past events can help you cleanse your memories and celebrate your path. By reframing these events or triggers, you will release blocked energy and create a space in which you can focus on your dreams. We'll go into this in more detail in chapter 3.

Are you going through a transition or a big change in your life? Changing careers, relationships, homes, or cities can send your heart and mind into a whirlwind of emotions that journaling will help you wade through. Getting married or having a baby is also a time of great transition that you'll want to capture in your journal as it is happening. Chapter 4 will explore how to use these transitions to gain knowledge and perspective and to honor your life.

Are there relationships in your life that can challenge your self-image? Are you feeling overwhelmed or frustrated? Would you like to connect more deeply to those around you? Chapter 5 will guide you in figuring out how the world is mirroring what's going on inside you. It will also help your life reflect the most wonderful aspects of yourself.

What do you feel is missing in your life? Are you searching for a significant relationship, the perfect job, or a new house? Are you struggling with finding your purpose, or do you lack passion in your life? Many times we must learn to feel complete and happy on our own before the right person or thing will show up in our lives. Using your journal to get really clear about what you are looking for will ensure that you are ready when the perfect person or situation shows up. Or maybe you know exactly what you want to create in your life, and you want to figure out the first steps to take. Creating a vision in your journal of what you want will help you attract the circumstances to manifest it. Chapter 6 will give you some great inspiration about how to do this.

Perhaps you are searching for a greater spiritual connection, or you want to cultivate your intuition or begin expressing yourself in a creative way. Chapter 7 will look at the link between creative inspiration and connecting to a higher power in your journal.

And finally, chapter 8 will guide you in using your journal for the rest of your life. Your journal can help you hold on to the moments of Divine inspiration and traverse the uncharted territory of your dreams.

No matter where you begin your journal, as you open yourself to your inner wisdom your path will become clearer and clearer.

Try This
Taking Stock

Take stock of your life. What is working? What isn't? Allow yourself to be completely honest in your description. What is overwhelming you? What do you love about yourself? Are you feeling jealous, angry, or envious of a friend, coworker, or celebrity? What's missing in your life? What makes your life full? Name the three best things in your life. Now name the worst. Consider this exercise a new starting point, in which you can get to know yourself and your desires. How will you ever have the life you long for if you can't pinpoint where you are today? Capture a little bit of your life at a time — little details, feelings, and situations that are going on at this moment. How does it feel to be you right now? How do you wish it would feel?

———————————

Here's a journal entry from a friend of mine, written just after she bought her first home:

> *Nothing's clear; my mind is tired tonight. I think about where I am in my life. Visions of men run through my mind; what do they mean to me? I work on fine-tuning myself, my house, my life. My nail polish is chipping off and I need to shave my legs, but I took the time to hang some pictures on the wall. Shave later, catch up on your manicure some other day. Today I will do things that have an immediate effect on me, my surroundings, something that will last. Nail polish chips, legs grow hairy, life moves on!*

"Nail polish chips, legs grow hairy, life moves on." These are words to live by! Your life is moving on right now. What are you going to do to craft and shape your life? Are you going to continue living your life as if you'll get started tomorrow, or next week, or next year? Carpe diem!

In the movie *Dead Poet's Society*, Robin Williams plays an inspiring poetry teacher who encourages his students as he reads from Whitman: "The powerful play goes on, and you may contribute a verse. What will your verse be?" What will *your* verse be? You get to answer that question, starting right now. No matter where you are in your life, your journal will be there for you as you contribute your verse to the world.

CHAPTER 3

Cleansing and Celebrating the Past

And though it's only ink that flows,
from wounds so deep inside of me,
I yearn to find out what ink knows, and so,
I write on ceaselessly.

— Dennis, age fifty-five, journaling for over thirty years

The fastest way to move forward in your life is to let go of the past. But how do you begin to let go? The first step is to recognize what emotions you've held inside. Only then can you determine the focus of your cleansing process and begin clearing out the junk. Understanding exactly what you are carrying around is essential; you may have to walk through your "stuff" to get to the other side.

Cleansing and celebrating the past in your journal is a practice. One long, impassioned journaling session probably won't change your life; it doesn't happen overnight. After all, it took most of your life for these emotions to build up inside you. But once you begin to purposefully cleanse yourself in your journal, you will almost certainly feel more serene immediately. Each time you write, you will feel the release of more pain and anger. Sometimes a new direction or answer will peek through. You may feel lighter after journaling, and you may remain more calm and peaceful in your daily life. This cleansing process will affect how you feel about the everyday pressures you experience. You will find yourself less reactive in stressful situations.

You may also notice that the universe continually brings you people and situations that give you the opportunity to cleanse yourself of the old stuff. If you can recognize and accept these gifts, you'll be able to let go of issues from your past that hold you back and channel the new energy into the life you choose to create.

Use the following activity to help you identify where you might be stuck.

Try This
Naming Your Emotions

At the top of a clean page in your journal, write "I feel angry." Then, for two full minutes, vent everything you feel angry about in your life. Then write "I feel sad," and go on venting for another two minutes. Select a third emotion to write about, and another after that, and then another. You will find that certain emotions bring up tons of immediate responses. Stay with the emotions that arise until you've written everything that comes to mind, then move on to the next emotion.

Refer to the following list of emotions for possible topics. Start with a few emotions from the left column, and end with some from the right column. The emotions in the right column will encourage you to look at the blessings or lessons learned from the difficult situations of the emotions in the left column. This can bring intuition to painful circumstances and help you tap into a greater plan or purpose for the challenges you face. The exercise will also allow you to end your journaling session feeling lighter and more joyful. Feel free to add your own! "I feel…"

Angry	Understanding
Sad	Loving
Afraid	Appreciative
Sorry	Grateful
Frustrated	Happy
Worried	Secure
Disappointed	Calm
Hurt	Courageous
Scared	Peaceful

You may have to do this cleansing exercise several times to feel really clear. Each time you do it, however, you'll notice that there is less negative emotion attached to the situations you're writing about. Perhaps you're wondering, "What if I'm afraid to feel a particular emotion?" Or maybe you're thinking, "I don't want to feel so much pain. It feels overwhelming." Don't worry. The easiest way to become free of an emotion is to let it flow onto the blank page.

Remember, it is perfectly normal to feel emotional as you write. Allow yourself to feel your pain or fear, and let it out. During timed writing exercises in my workshops, we often hear sniffles as people begin their writing. It is natural to want to immediately shut this off. Try to give yourself some space to release the emotions. It's okay to cry. If you let yourself write and cry for a few minutes, you will feel a sense of relief afterward.

While you are naming your emotions, you can also imagine that the emotions flowing through you are colors. Pick a color that makes sense to you. Anger, for instance, could be red. Sadness could be blue. Then visualize this color coursing throughout your body, swirling inside of you. As your pen touches the paper, or your fingers tap the keyboard, feel this color pouring out of your fingertips. The emotion is draining out of your body and onto the page.

What can you expect as you vent your emotions? Your head might feel lighter. You may find that your heart doesn't feel as heavy as it did moments ago. You might experience a tingling sensation that feels like a cool white light buzzing around your body. Imagine this white, clear, pure energy cleansing you as you write.

Dig a Little Deeper

The past can hold great trauma and triumph, depending on your perspective. When I began journaling, I was trying to figure out my past. My father left when I was seven years old. At the age of twenty-one, I realized that I still had a lot of anger toward him, and it was affecting every aspect of my life. I searched for a way to let it go.

I turned to my journal for help. For many years, I wrote angry letters to my father in my journals, such as this one:

Dear Dad,

Ha! How strange it feels to even write that name. I don't remember ever writing it before, not even on cards or presents when I was young. That name does not have a face for me, especially not associated with you. You are merely a sperm that gave me life. No more. How does that feel? Do you hurt? Are you lonely for a loving child to care for you in your older years? I'm better off without you. You mean nothing to me. You made me different. Thanks to you, on my wedding day it will be only me walking down the aisle, just like I've walked myself through life, without you. Surviving.

Did you even love me? Did you not feel any responsibility for me? Did you ever wonder where I was, what I was thinking, and what kind of person I turned out to be? My therapist told me that I will eventually come to know that I loved you very much and that you hurt me, but I don't really feel that now. I only feel anger.

As I wrote these letters, I began to understand that when my father left I packed all of my emotions into neat little boxes inside myself as a defense mechanism. Writing the letters to my father in a journal helped me begin to open those boxes. I was able to release the bottled-up pain and anger onto the blank pages, and after writing a letter I always felt lighter and less emotional.

Try This
Letter

Pick someone to write a letter to. It could be a parent, a family member, a former employer, or a lover. Pick someone you would have a hard time expressing yourself with face-to-face. You don't have to start with the most difficult person; just pick anyone and write a letter.

You never have to show this person the letter you write. In fact, you can rip it up and throw it away as soon as you are finished. I just want you to feel the stuff you've been holding back and let it dump onto the paper.

After you've finished writing your letter, take a deep breath and notice how you feel. Do you feel calmer or lighter? Does your heart feel more open? Do you have more you need to write? This is a great exercise to use any time you are feeling overwhelming emotions toward someone.

Shrinking Your Buttons

Do you ever feel as if you have giant buttons on your forehead, and anyone can come along and press them — sometimes with the tiniest effort? Can a seemingly small incident send you into a fury of anxiety and overanalysis? When you repress or swallow your emotions, hiding them away instead of dealing with them directly, they often show up later in the form of specific triggers (or "buttons") that set off a range of strong emotions. Your journal is the perfect place to take a closer look at these bottled-up emotions.

Once you've identified some of your buttons, you will be able to shrink them. You may never get rid of them completely, but you can reduce their size, making it more difficult for others to bump into your buttons and ruin your day.

Here is a journal entry written by Debbie, mother of seven-year-old Gwynn, on a day when her buttons got pushed:

Something is unraveling somewhere. I seem to be dealing with ignorance and irrationality from every direction! I got into a fight with the office manager at Gwynn's school today over some simple paperwork that was accidentally left out of her file. Then I tried to make a doctor's appointment and they can't see me until September — no exceptions. After an extremely stressful morning, I found myself yelling at the poor man behind the counter at the gas station. My blood felt like it was boiling over! Am I doing something to attract these struggles into my life? What is my lesson here? How can I learn to control my anger and not take it out on those around me? What is really going on here? I feel like I run into mean, angry people everywhere I turn.

Have you ever had one of those days? It feels like the world is out to get you. You seem to remember starting the day out in a fairly good mood, minding your own business, doing your thing, but chaos and craziness are now chasing you from location to location, ruining your day. I would like to suggest that when a day goes off course to this degree, it's a good idea to stop and take a look at your buttons.

Try This

Look Closely at Your Buttons

What exactly has you so upset? Retrace your day and look at the first moment when the tension began to rise and you pushed it back down. It probably wasn't just one thing that set you off; it was probably a series of events that built up until you blew your top. As you unload some of these pent-up emotions in your journal, look for a word or phrase that describes what seems to be happening. "No one wants to help me!" "I have to fight this bureaucracy." "They're wrong and I'm right!" "I'm so overwhelmed." Search for phrasing that resonates most deeply for you, and try to connect to a time when you felt that way in your past. Your buttons didn't get created overnight. They usually represent something you've come up against over and over in your life, and that's why your reaction feels so strong. You are not only reacting to the snippy sales clerk, but the way your second-grade teacher coldly dismissed you, or the grandmother who be-rated you for not following directions. These emotions are still hanging on inside of you, just waiting for the opportu-nity to rise up and get revenge.

Identifying the old emotions and dumping them into your journal lightens your load. The lighter you feel, the more joyful your journey will be.

Completing Your Incompletions

Many relationships and events in our lives leave us feeling incomplete. We may feel "I should have..." or "I wish I'd..." Sometimes we carry these unresolved emotions into other situations in our present life. Our anger explodes onto our children when they leave a giant mess, when it's actually the child inside of us that's feeling overwhelmed. Or we blame a meddling mother-in-law for creating problems within our marriage, when actually we are at fault for repeating scenarios we watched over and over as a child in our own home. Until we allow ourselves to feel resolved or complete with past relationships and events, we will create new situations to give ourselves the opportunity to heal.

These days, many people are making a commitment to stop destructive family cycles. Journaling can be your best tool for quieting the madness in your head and preventing it from manifesting in your life. Resolving past situations and relationships in your journals today will lead to a happier, healthier you right now.

Try This
Completing Your Incompletions

An *incompletion* is any relationship or event about which you have unresolved feelings. If you ran into a person you feel incomplete with on the street, it would feel uncomfortable. There would be things you need to say to, or hear from, that person. If there is an event you feel incomplete about, you feel conflicted and emotional when you reminisce about it.

In order to complete an incompletion, you need to write a healing vision of it.

Make a list of your incompletions. Pick a person or event from your list of incompletions and write about it. Write in detail what you remember and how you feel about it. You don't have to be "fair" in your description; you can allow yourself to rant and rave. This writing is only for you.

If the incompletion concerns a person, once you've gotten all your emotions onto the page write a letter to yourself from him or her saying the exact things that will make you feel better. Perhaps this would be an apology or an affirmation of love. If your incompletion concerns an event, revise the scenario. Rewrite it the way you would have liked it to go. Allow yourself to feel clear inside.

Writing about people and events that distress you releases negative energy onto the page, diffusing its force. The tension and anger, sadness and frustration can flow directly from your heart through your pen. With the flow of ink across the paper, your negative emotions come pouring out of you, through your arms and out your fingertips, freeing you from your past and allowing you to move closer to the life of your dreams.

A workshop participant once said to me, "But my list of incompletions could fill my whole journal!" My response was, "Why not? Who cares? That's perfectly okay." When I began journaling, I felt the same way. Please don't be overwhelmed by making this list. It's a starting point. As you clear people and events from your list, your newfound clarity and

peace of mind will probably spill over into other areas of
your life. Things will just fall off your list. Remember, healing is an evolutionary process; with each writing session, it
will become easier to move through the cleansing process.

Recognizing Inner Wisdom

Most of us spend much of our lives searching for love and
answers outside ourselves, when everything we really want
can be found within. Journaling can end this fruitless search
by putting us back in touch with our answers and our inner
wisdom. It's easy to feel overwhelmed and confused on a
daily basis when we're out of touch with our intuition or
inner wisdom. There are so many messages coming toward
us every day from families, friends, society, and the media;
they tell us who they think we should be, how we should act
or react, and what to do with our lives. Your journal gives
you a place to let your inner wisdom guide you. Ask the
questions that are confusing you and listen for the answers.
You may only hear a whisper at first, but as you pay more
attention, your intuition will get stronger and louder.

When Ellen (age twenty-eight) did this exercise in one
of my workshops, she began to recognize the wisdom that
existed inside her. In the following journal entry, Ellen acknowl-
edges a period of self-destructive behavior in her past:

Dear Ellen,

   It feels weird writing your name. I know how you hated your
   name back then. It isn't so bad, you know. Things aren't always

*as bad as they seem. You needed love and I couldn't give it to you,
so you had no choice but to go outside for it. It became an obses-
sive addiction to get others to acknowledge, like, and love you. But
I do love you.*

*I am sorry I tried to kill us off. I was out of control. I
wanted us to be happy and in a place where we would be loved
unconditionally. I wanted help.*

*I have let you keep your misguided perceptions for a very
long time. It has clouded a lot of things for us. Do you want us
to grow and be loved? Yes. Then we need to join together and open
up our heart and let our love overflow. But we have a lot of stuff
to clear up inside. If we open our heart, it will be forced to clear.
You are never alone or without love. I am here for you, always.
The love is inside of you.*

Love, Ellen

As Ellen dialogued with the little girl inside her, a wise
woman showed up, telling her, "You are never alone or without love. I am here for you, always." Like Ellen, we all must
learn to give ourselves what we'd like to receive from the outside world. When we journal, we channel the power to heal
anything that still hurts us.

Try This
Heal and Celebrate

Even painful memories can be transformed by the ability to
nurture yourself within your journal. Try to identify at least

five major turning points in your life. List the strengths you've gained from these events. Write about how these events impacted your life and the person you have become. Celebrate the gifts you've been given through your experiences. The gifts you recognize today are the gifts you were meant to share with the world.

Now, looking to the future, what would make you feel loved, peaceful, and happy? Begin to visualize how you want to feel and what you want to do on a daily basis. Give your inner wisdom a voice. There is a place inside you that holds great dreams. Your passion lives there, as well. Start trusting your instincts, and write the first thing that comes to you. Allow the wisest part of you to write an inspiring vision for your life.

The Pen and the Art of Forgiveness

One evening, seven years after I wrote the first angry letter to my father, I sat down with my journal. I had nothing particular in mind to write about, but to my surprise forgiveness poured onto the page.

> *Dear Doug,*
>
> *This is going to be a tough letter. It is something I have thought about doing for a long time. But I guess I was afraid...*

As my pen moved across the pages of my journal, I knew that this letter to my father would be *the one*. I had written so many letters to him over the years, never with any intention of sending them, but this one was different. This was the letter I would mail:

> ...*My heart is pounding, just trying to form the words on the paper. You can't imagine how many times I've written letters to you in my journals, looking for answers to be channeled through my hand onto the paper. But this one is different; this one I will send to you. I am thirty-two years old, and I have two beautiful daughters and a wonderful husband, but there seems to be a hole somewhere deep down that I just can't patch up by myself. Where do I begin?*
>
> *All my life, I've said, "My parents' divorce was for the best." That's what I had been told. "Everything's okay." And I think I believed it for a long time — most of my life.*
>
> *I remember standing in a bookstore when I was twenty-one years old and picking up a book about adult children of divorce. There was a quote on the back cover — a girl talking about the pain she felt inside over her parents' divorce, and describing how she still feels incredibly sad. She said that your whole childhood is your parents, and that if something happens to that union — the world shatters and is never quite right again. It then said that the woman was fifty-six years old when she wrote this. Tears began streaming down my face, and I realized for the first time how much pain I had inside.*
>
> *That was over ten years ago. I've done a lot of soul-searching — a lot of reading and journaling and talking — trying to get in touch with that little girl inside of me who still carries the pain.*
>
> *I am in a better place in my life now. I want you to know who I am. I want you to know what incredible granddaughters*

you have. They are just amazing! And I believe that we are really great parents. I know that working through all of my feelings about the divorce has helped me to be a better mother. But there is still a little girl inside me who wants to ask all the questions that were never answered. She still feels lost and alone and insecure. She needed her Daddy, and he wasn't there.

I don't want anything from you. I have thought of picking up the phone a hundred times — but these are not things I could say to you over the phone. There are so many questions I would want to ask you — but could not.

Writing like this feels safe to me because I've written you so many letters in my journals, with no intention of ever sending them. I want to know who you are and what you were going through back then. I'd like to hear your perspective, adult-to-adult.

Maybe you would like to meet your granddaughters.

I would like to talk to you, but I am not attached to a specific vision. If it's meant to be, it will be. I believe that you did the best you could with what you knew at the time. I would really like to know who you are now.

Sandy

I was so proud of that letter. I showed it to everyone who walked in my front door. But the letter sat on my kitchen counter, addressed and stamped, for over two months. In the letter, I'd told my father that I'd forgiven him, and I believed that I had — until one night when I wrote a question in my journal.

I never used to pay much attention to my dreams. But a good friend encouraged me to write a question in my journal to be answered in my dreams, so I tried it. My question was a variation of something I've been asking my entire life: "What is my purpose? Please guide me. Help me focus my energy for the higher good." I left the journal open on my nightstand so that my question would be answered while I slept.

The dream I had was very specific. I was sitting in a therapist's office, and the therapist was holding a list of significant people in my life (parents, siblings, friends, relatives). As she scanned the list, she said, "Now, we are going to do an exercise in forgiveness. I want you to repeat after me, 'I forgive you, so-and-so.'" She scanned the list. "Okay, let's just start. I forgive you…" (she randomly picked a name from the list) "…Doug Johnson." I could feel a lump growing in my throat, and my eyes stung with tears. I couldn't speak. Why couldn't she have picked someone else? Why did she have to start with my father? I couldn't speak, and I began to cry hysterically. My shoulders heaved up and down as I gasped for the next breath.

The therapist, shaking her head, looked me straight in the eyes and said, "Sandy, you have not forgiven your father. I want you to go home and journal. Make a list of all the things you need to forgive your father for."

I awoke from the dream stunned, but I faithfully wrote down every detail I could remember from the dream. It needed no interpretation; it was painfully clear. The reason I had not mailed my father's letter was because I had not truly forgiven him. So I immediately did the forgiveness exercise my dream therapist had given me:

I forgive you, Doug Johnson. I forgive you for never being there when I needed you. I forgive you for never calling or sending cards on my birthdays. I forgive you for not seeing how much pain you left in your wake. I forgive you for leaving behind three little children who thought you were their world. I forgive you for hurting me so badly...

I wrote over three pages of "I forgive you's" in my journal. They poured out of me. Then an incredible thing happened. I heard a voice in my head. It said, "Mail the letter." So I wrote that down.

Then I wrote, "Why do I have to mail the letter? What will that really do?"

The response came: "Mail the letter. It is symbolic. It will set you free — free to move past this pain and anger, free to get on with your life, free to be who you truly are."

I walked downstairs and picked up the letter. As the sun rose, I placed the letter in the mailbox. I immediately felt a little lighter in my footsteps, like I was walking two inches above the ground. It was as if I had taken twenty years of pain and anger and stuffed it in the mailbox. Even if I never received a response from my father, I felt complete with him. He would finally know who I am and the healing I have done. The letter left nothing unsaid.

My father did call two weeks later. We shared an awkward and uncomfortable conversation. He couldn't bring himself to talk about the letter. Still, I felt clear. I felt complete. I felt Divinely guided. My father knew me through my letter.

Try This
Forgiveness

This cleansing exercise works fabulously when you are holding anger toward someone who caused you pain, left you, or
even died. It is easy. Write "I forgive you..." followed by a
specific person's name. Then list all the things for which you
feel the need to forgive that person. Use this activity to forgive yourself or others and to let go of negative energy that's
holding you back.

Forgiveness is not something you do for another person. You do it for yourself to free yourself. Although you
may not believe it's working at the moment when you're
doing it, each time you write the words "I forgive you
for...[fill in the blank]" on the page, your heart will get a
little lighter and your pent-up emotions will begin to evap-
orate. Once you begin to forgive, or at least reach a state of
acceptance about the past, you will attract the good things
you want into your life and start living more peacefully and
joyfully today.

I encourage you to practice forgiveness in your journals to
release yourself. It takes a tremendous amount of energy
to carry around anger, hatred, disappointment, frustration,
and sadness. Everywhere you go, you carry these emotions,
holding them inside your body. Forgiveness allows you to
release that heavy, negative energy and move into a new

day feeling lighter and more focused. Eventually the old emotions will no longer cloud your vision. You will be free to move past them and become who you truly are.

Try This
Ask a Question

Do you pay attention to your dreams? Do you give them significance in your life?

Keeping a dream log can connect you to a greater plan for your life. It can answer questions that are troubling you, point you in a new direction, or help you make a decision.

Write a question in your journal just before you go to bed, then leave your journal open on your nightstand. Reread the question a couple of times before turning off the lights, and ask that the answer be revealed in your dreams. As soon as you awaken, even if it's still dark, write down anything you remember about your dreams. You don't even have to turn the lights on; just scratch out a few sentences to be remembered in the morning. Before you get out of bed, write down the details of the dream as specifically as possible. Don't try to interpret the dream yet; just write down all the details you can recall.

After you've captured the essence of the dream in your journal, go back and read your question again. Then read your description of the dream with your question in mind. Do any sentences jump out at you from your written version of the dream? Are there any symbols that point you in a certain direction? Use your intuition to figure out what your dream could be telling you.

There are many books that can help you interpret your dreams. Some people believe that every person in your dream represents an aspect of yourself. Listing the outstanding qualities of people in your dreams can give you a clue about what your subconscious may be trying to tell you. Or you may want to interpret the symbols in your dreams. For example, shoes may represent a foundation or something you stand on, a core belief. Water can represent your life: was it smooth sailing, rough, or calm? Read your dream to a friend for an outside intuitive impression. Have fun!

Letting Go

Two months after my dream revelation, my father finally met his granddaughters. My sister and I call our trip "The Healing Journey." We packed my two little girls into a rented minivan and took off to meet my father. We drove, we sang, we ate. The girls screamed, and finally they slept.

As we approached the city where my father lived, I began to panic. My heart was pounding. I attempted to convince my sister to turn around. But she was determined. If she had not been with me, I never would have made it. I did not want to go. I did not want to look into his eyes and smile.

We pulled into the gas station where we had agreed to rendezvous, and there was my dad. His brown hair had turned white. He looked much shorter than my young memory had painted him. We exchanged pleasantries and then went out for dinner.

The girls had a fantastic time dancing around the empty dance floor as the jukebox played. I cautiously attempted to begin a *real* conversation with my father. "So, what did you think of my letter?" I asked. His kind blue eyes smiled at me, "I'd like to talk to you about it, but now is not the time." My heart sank. As I stared into his face, I saw traces of my own. I also saw the many hard years etched around those blue eyes. I knew that this man had given me life — that he had been part of the grand plan that created me. But I also realized that this was all I would ever get from him. Perhaps he was afraid, maybe he felt guilty. I do not know.

On this journey, I saw very clearly how different my life would have been if my parents had stayed together. I realized that the universe has a plan for us all, and healing the little girl inside me from the pain of my parents' divorce was a big part of my plan. In that moment, sitting across from this stranger who had my eyes, with a confusing, forced familiarity engulfing us, I realized that this would have to be enough. I took in a deep breath, and I let it all go once again. After dinner, I said good-bye to my father and we drove away.

It was not the storybook ending I'd been hoping for — not the long, deep, healing conversation I had envisioned. It was only a woman-child, who is now a wife and mother, letting go of an imaginary father figure — free to move past the pain and anger, free to get on with her life, free to be who she really is.

I realized that I had been waiting my entire life for this imaginary father figure to show up on his white horse and fill the hole he left in my heart. He was never coming. I also realized that, even if he did become a regular part of our lives — Sunday dinners, holiday gifts, and all the rest —

that wasn't going to fill me up. In fact, nothing out there would fill me up — not my husband or my children or my career or a new house. I had to figure out how to fill myself up, and my journal was the place to start.

When I reflect on past journal entries, I realize that the woman who wrote those first angry letters never could have forgiven. Journaling changed who I am and how I view the world. It helped me emerge from being the young girl I was, filled with anger and confusion, completely out of touch with her true self, into being a woman who could hear the messages from her soul: "Mail the letter. It will set you free."

Mailing that letter to my father and forcing myself to get a bit of closure on our relationship freed energy inside me for doing other things with my life, such as writing this book. It didn't happen overnight, just like getting to a place where I could forgive my father didn't happen overnight. It takes time and writing and allowing your emotions to flow into your journals, attempting to make sense of it all and to gain a larger perspective on your life.

During my own healing journey, I've written many letters and poems and done many cleansing exercises. I've dumped my emotions onto the pages of countless journals over the course of many years, looking for *me*.

Many times, the journal entries were triggered by some unwitting person who happened to bump into one of my buttons. These people and situations allowed me to cleanse my anger and pain a little more. Each time I grabbed my journal, upset about something "out there," I realized that it was always about what was inside of me. That is all that really matters: what lives inside each of us. Every time you write, you get a little closer to your true self. Each time you sit down with a journal, your inner wisdom has a chance to speak to you.

You can't give of yourself completely until you've cleansed your past. Journaling allows you to step out of the details of your history and see the grand plan. How will these events contribute to the larger picture of your life?

Once you've dumped all the crap and clatter that races through your head, the wise person who lives deep inside has a voice in your journal. Your mind becomes quiet, and you can hear the messages of your soul.

Healing Is a Slightly Messy Process

I wish I could tell you that if you follow the steps I've laid out, you will be entirely cleansed and permanently healed, and that by the time you've finished this book you will live happily ever after. But in my experience, the healing process isn't quite so linear. It's not a clean, step-by-step process; it constantly flows in and out and through our lives. My joys and triumphs have always been sandwiched between my cleansing and healing experiences. It is still this way.

Journaling has not made my life perfect. I don't believe there is such a thing as a perfect life. But my journaling practice has put me in touch with who I truly am and what I was meant to do with my life. The experiences that show up on the pages of my journals sometimes seem magical. They are also merely reflections of a normal life. Likewise, your life is magical now, although you may not have realized it yet. Your journal will reveal this to you.

We've begun to explore how to cleanse the clutter in your head and heal what's happened in the past. In the next chapter, we will address the major life transitions that force us to examine and reexamine who we are and who we want to be. This will set the stage for beginning the process of using our journals to create a life of joy and abundance.

CHAPTER 4

Expectations and Major Life Transitions

They say we pray to God when the foundations of our lives are shaking, only to discover that God is the one shaking them. Going through any big change in life — leaving home, getting married, breaking up, having kids, losing a job, or relocating — can shake us up. Does change rattle your self-confidence and make your insides flutter? You're not the only one. But big change can be a big blessing. What is it about change that sends our humanness into overdrive? Why do we question ourselves during times of transition, wondering whether or not we can handle the next day or even the next moment?

We are creatures of habit. Our routines ground us and give us the illusion that we are in control of our lives. We feel safer when we know what the next day holds. But though we feel better without unexpected circumstances popping up and getting in the way of our plans, living in complete safety and control can get a little boring. In the movie *Parenthood,* life is compared to a rollercoaster — a ride that can make you frightened, scared, sick, excited, thrilled, and happy, all at the same time. If you could design your life more like a merry-go-round, would you? Just going around and around, the same thing around every turn, no surprises, no changes or transitions? Life would get pretty boring without any variation or evolution.

Some people love surprises and thrive on the unknown. My friend Sara told me that she loves change. "The bigger the better! Bring it on! What's so great about the past?" However, for many people change represents strange and unfamiliar territory that can be a source of stress.

Your journal can be an extremely helpful tool for helping you embrace the unpredictable path of your life. Let's take a look at some of the kinds of life transitions for which journaling can be useful.

Career Changes

We spend a large percentage of our time at work, so switching careers or losing a job usually means we're in for some big changes.

It's the first day of your new career! You have your new suit on, along with your freshly ironed shirt, new briefcase, and pen. The butterflies are dancing in your belly. The future is bright, yet uncertain. Starting over in a new place surrounded by unfamiliar faces can be exciting and unsettling. Writing about these feelings in your journal can help calm you down. Are you feeling like the new kid on the block, left out or maybe a little overwhelmed? Are you worried that you might not live up to expectations and job performance standards?

Or perhaps you've lost your job and feel as if you'll never get another one. The money pressures are growing, and you are imagining how it will feel to be evicted from your apartment or to have your car repossessed. Your worries are spiraling out of control. If you dump your concerns out on the page, they begin to lose their power over you. Give the journal a chance to help you work it out. Once you freely express your worrisome feelings, you can begin to give yourself the kind of sunny encouragement that just can't break through when your head is clouded with anxiety. A better perspective is sure to show up, helping you see a clear path rather than wallowing in fear.

Try This

CEO: Chief of Emotions Officer

Focus on the career changes you are going through. You may have grand plans for these transitions. Do you see yourself working your way up through the corporation and becoming the CEO? Or would you like to gain some valuable experience and strike out in your own business? Have you set goals for your performance in the coming months? Build yourself up by writing all the congratulatory phrases you would love to hear from your superiors. Write about how proud you are of yourself — or how scared you are. If you are still in the middle of the interview process, imagine yourself having several job offers from desirable companies. While changing jobs or careers can be stressful, it is also a fresh beginning — a chance to reinvent your life. Use your journal to write about all the things you would like to attract into your life. Let yourself unload, dumping your emotions onto the page. Write anything. Nothing is off limits.

Another effective technique for gaining a better perspective is dialoguing with your inner wisdom (or a higher energy, or God). Here's a journal entry from David, who was having a conversation with his inner wisdom during a difficult time in his life:

> *Work* — *I am out of work, unemployed, again.*
>
> *You are never out of what you call "work."*
>
> *Well, I know I always "work." My soul is always undertaking that which I came here to do.*
>
> *So why are you so concerned with employment?*
>
> *Fear.*
>
> *Yes, fear. That is what your "work" is about, is it not? Hasn't most of your life been a battle with fear?*
>
> *Yes.*

So, here it is again. Asking. Waiting.
Waiting? For what?
To be loved by you.
Why?
So that it can come home.
Why does it need me?
You created it.
Why?
You were curious.

David told me that dialoguing with his inner wisdom, or Spirit, keeps him coming back to his journal. He can hear a voice that is not always present in his daily thoughts. The journal turns up the volume on this wise voice. Today, David is the successful owner of Changing Times Books & Gifts in West Palm Beach, Florida. This wonderful store carries, among other things, hundreds of beautiful journals. David's passion for his work is apparent the moment you walk in the door.

When I first began teaching journaling workshops, I had to make the leap from thinking about doing it to actually picking up the phone and calling the manager of my local bookstore to ask if they wanted to hear about the journalution. I had a vision that I wanted to inspire millions of people to use journaling as a tool to heal and to manifest their dreams, but I hadn't actually done anything about it yet. What if they said no? What if they laughed at me?

At moments like that, when the doubt begins to surface, it's a great time to do a dialoguing exercise such as the one David used.

Try This
Dialoguing

Have a conversation with the critical voice in your mind. Listen to all the doubts and fears that seem to be ready and waiting to pounce on your dreams. Then bring another voice into the dialogue: a supportive, wise voice. Use that voice to give yourself some encouragement, just as you would encourage a dear friend or family member who was going through self-doubt. Let the critic and the supporter talk back and forth until the critic begins to soften. Allow yourself to anticipate victory, see it, and feel it. Paint a picture in your journal of your dreams coming true. See yourself as powerful and capable of accomplishing this task, as well as many more even greater feats. Take a deep breath and tell yourself that you *can* do it. There is nothing stopping you unless you allow it to.

Moving Out into the Real World

Do you remember what it felt like the first time you lived on your own? What's more thrilling — or scarier — than being completely independent for the first time in your life? It's the most exciting thing in the world, and yet it can feel pretty overwhelming. I remember thinking that college was going to be like a summer camp. On being dropped off, I couldn't wait for my mother to get out of the dorm so I could hang out with my friends. No curfew! No rules! It didn't take long for the realization to sink in that my family was hundreds of miles away and I was sharing a small room with a complete stranger.

A journal is the perfect companion to have by your side at every twist and turn of this adventure. It's there for you when you are juggling friends, new responsibilities, and difficult situations. The real world is full of friends, fun, new experiences, and having to act like you've got it all together. In those moments when it seems like you'll never have it figured out, your journal is the perfect place to turn.

When you're older, it will be lovely to reminisce about what the enthusiastic, spontaneous, open-minded young person you are now was thinking about the world. Your journal doesn't have to be just words, either. You can draw pictures, paste photos, make collages, and tape mementos into your journal. Scrapbooking has become so popular that there are now entire stores dedicated to supplies and inspirations for putting together these beautiful books. Try combining journal entries with your scrapbooks. Write little notes about thoughts and feelings that go along with the items. Experiment with your journal, and visit one of these scrapbook supply stores for inspiration.

In her book *Spilling Open*, Sabrina Ward Harrison shares her journal/scrapbook of her life between the ages of eighteen and twenty-one. She describes feeling disconnected from her body and feeling watched. Ms. Harrison's wisdom surfaces in her journal and offers a gem for us all, young and old:

If I was to have an answer to this growing pain question it would be something like this: You've got this amazing creature — yourself. That can move and breathe, dance and cry. And you have a certain amount of moments. And you have this chance to do absolutely anything; to dance on the roof in euphoria and pray beside the ocean. We have the chance every moment to be alive and to give to this world, who needs each one of us so badly.[1]

Try This

Inspiration for Your Journal

Gather a few magazines, markers, crayons, scissors, and old photographs around you on a table. Flip through the magazines looking for words or pictures that inspire you or that express exactly what you are feeling right now. Clip out at least five things. Turn to a blank page in your journal and use the crayons and markers to make a backdrop, or just begin writing using different colors for different letters and words. Cut your old photographs, magazine pictures, or clipped-out words to fit into the journal entry. Just the eyes or lips or laughing faces can be glued or taped all over the page or in between the words to help express yourself in this moment. There is no wrong way to do this. Let yourself revert to being seven years old. Have fun! This is a great project to do with children; they will love to create their own journal entry, too.

I wish I'd discovered my passion for journaling earlier in life. I would love to go back now and read what that young girl was thinking and feeling. Did life turn out as she hoped and planned? It is such an important time in life, stepping out and discovering who you will be. If these moments and decisions are not written down, they will be forgotten. The act of writing ensures that these occasions will be waiting for you when you are ready to look back on your journey and make sense of it all.

When the newness of being on your own is over and you have survived out in the "real world," your journal will still be there to guide you through your next big decisions and transitions.

Gain Perspective on Change

Our life circumstances are constantly changing. But as an unknown author wrote, "If nothing ever changed, there would be no butterflies." Journaling while going through a major life transition can help you gain perspective on the situation. Finding out who we truly are and who we want to be is an evolutionary process in which we can take part. We don't have to be like a paper bag being tossed about in a storm. We can take the helm and steer our lives in the direction of our dreams.

Unlike that paper bag blowing around, we can take action on our own behalf, and even possibly redirect the forces that push on us. In life, things happen that we have no control over, but we can always control how we react and the next steps we take. Use your journal to consider your options and check in with your intuition before taking your next step. Make sure your inner wisdom is guiding you. Your major life transition may be completely joyful, or it may seem as if your whole world has come crashing down around you. Your journal is the wise friend who will guide you through, helping to keep your head about you and your feet on the ground while giving you a vision for the greatest life you can imagine. Your journal will also help you devise a road map of how to get there. (We'll talk more about that in chapter 6: Hopes, Dreams, and Visions.)

Try This
You as the Hero

At the top of a journal page, write the prompt "What have been the three biggest changes in my life?" Then describe three significant transitions that have occurred in your life. Reflect on how these changes felt as they were happening. What kind of person were you before going through each change or transition? How do these experiences affect you now? What qualities or strengths did you discover in yourself during these transitions? View your life from a higher perspective. Imagine your life as a movie: How did these events move you closer to being the hero of your life's movie? What could you do now that would help create a vision for living the life you long for?

Primary Relationships

The cute guy in the elevator asked you out. You met your soul mate. He popped the question! She said yes! You have dreamed of this day your entire life. You are so happy! Now what? Well, first…pick up a pen and write down every detail. Yes, yes, you will remember this moment forever. But, trust me, you'll be thankful that you took the time to record the exact thoughts and images that are floating around in your head. Write about the music, the weather, the smells, and what you were wearing. (Men, I know you probably don't care one bit what you were wearing when you met the love of your life. Ladies, feel free to describe the delicate lavender frock and the way the breeze was blowing through your hair, just like on the cover of a magazine.) Think of these types of journal entries as internal snapshots. Tape a card from the restaurant in your journal, or the tickets from the theater, or draw a picture of something from the experience: hearts around your loved one's name, or maybe two stick figures standing at the ocean kissing. You get the idea.

A new relationship means the beginning of a new type of family. This person will meet your friends and relatives. Having a journal by your side to help you navigate the multitude of situations, suggestions, lists, tasks, and well-intentioned advice will help you cement your union from a state of calm and centered clarity.

Here's a journal entry from Mya, who was caught up in hectic wedding plans:

*I've lost touch with myself, with God, and with so many people.
I'm too scared to write. I know that if I write, the truth will
come pouring out. What is the truth?*

*The truth is that I stepped out of my boundaries, way out.
I dove headfirst into too many things: relationships, work, spending — lots of spending. I've lived most of my life impulsively,
without thinking.*

*I want to tell my parents, "Let's forget the big wedding. Let's
just have a small get-together." I hear the stress in my mom's
voice. I bought a very expensive dress. What was I thinking? It's
too much glamour and pretentiousness.*

*I'm just absorbing life like a sponge. My sponge is full now —
too full — and my spirit is dripping from the weight. I'm confused;
that's where things lie. I haven't committed fully. I have completely
given up planning, and I have given up my word. I'm scared shit-
less about getting married. Is this really what is right for me?*

I recently spoke with Mya, and she did get married in
Puerto Rico at her family's home six months later. She said
that, as they exited the church amidst bubbles being blown
by friends and family, she took a deep breath and finally
relaxed. Mya said she looked around the reception and saw
guests who had traveled from far away to be with them on
their special day. She remembered all the dreams she had
as a little girl of her wedding day: the moment she entered
the church and everyone turned to see her in the wedding
dress, her father lifting the veil from her face, her first dance
with her new husband.

Mya is now three months pregnant with their first
daughter. "I laughed so hard when I reread that journal entry,"

she told me. "I am in such a different place right now. I am very grateful that I wrote it all down. The little stuff does count, but it all works out. I got myself so worked up about all the details, but in the end it's the memories of being with friends and family and celebrating together that matter most. Keeping a journal through the beginnings of a relationship, engagement, and wedding planning helps you remember all the little amazing moments that just slip by otherwise."

Try This

How Do I Love Thee?

Make a list of all the reasons why you love and care about your beloved. Write about his laugh, about how you see a reflection of your best self in his eyes, and the way you feel as if you've come home when you are with him. Describe her grace as she moves across the room and how your heart races when you hear her voice. Keep this list close to your heart in case you become overwhelmed by the relationship, or in case engagement and wedding preparations threaten to kidnap your sanity. Include funny stories and private jokes that only the two of you share. Continue to add to the list through-out your first months and years together. Hand-write this list on fancy paper and present it to your lover on a special anniversary or on your wedding night.

Using a journal as you are navigating a new relationship will keep you connected to what is truly important to you and your special someone. Okay, maybe not every single moment will be calm and centered. Still, keeping a journal can definitely help you appreciate the special moments. And it can bring you a lifetime of memories as you capture the moments of beginning your lives together.

Expecting Transformations

Expecting a baby can be one of the most transformative events in any parent's life. If you keep a journal through this time, it can later take you back to the time "before baby" that is almost impossible to remember once your little bundle of joy arrives. It will also be a great documentation of those foggy early years, filled with sleep deprivation and 3:00 A.M. feedings. Here's a journal entry from my first pregnancy:

> *I am beginning this journal as one person, knowing that I will be a very different person as I complete these pages. I am going to be a mother. Wow. That feels so strange. It's the first time I've actually seen it written down on paper. It is truly amazing that I have this little person growing inside me — a person who is going to change my life like nothing I could ever dream of.*
>
> *I can't wait to meet you, watch you grow and become your own person — independent, strong, and confident. I know I'll make mistakes, and I hope you will forgive me. I just want you to have the self-confidence that I did not have as a child.*
>
> *For today, I will take very good care of you and protect you while you are growing inside me, preparing for your life outside. I will enjoy this transition from just Sandy to Sandy the mom.*

(Wow!) I'll nurture you and myself and watch in amazement what happens over the next nine months.

We know that keeping scrapbooks or photo albums can be a wonderful gift passed down from generation to generation, but I often imagine a young woman, perhaps my granddaughter, finding my journals when she is pregnant with her first child and discovering that all mothers-to-be have some feelings of inadequacy and uncertainty. "Will I be able to do this?" "I feel lost and unsure. I don't know what to do next." As she reads these words, she will take comfort in them and feel more compassion for herself. I imagine that knowing her grandmother or great-great-grandmother had the same tentative thoughts about her own life will give her some sense of peace. Sharing our journeys and transitions with our ancestors connects us in a way that goes beyond a family tree. We are giving the gift of our souls and leaving behind a trace of our true nature, more than could ever be captured in a photograph.

Here's a great exercise to try no matter where you are in your life. It will be a wonderful moment to look back and reflect on and a beautiful gift to give to your loved ones in the future.

Try This
Who Am I Now?

Write the prompt "Who am I now?" at the top of a page, set a timer for ten minutes, and start writing. Your journaling doesn't have to be chronological. It doesn't have to make any sense. It can be jumbled thoughts mixed together on the page, one after another. The point is to get lost in the act of writing. If your mind jumps to another subject, just follow it.

Now see yourself at the age of eight, then sixteen, then twenty-five. Who were you then? Describe the differences between who you were and who you are becoming. How will the coming months and years transform your life? Then describe the *you* that has always been here. What is that person's vision of your life? How has she or he guided you? Have you been listening, or have you been living on autopilot? When was the last time you checked in with the inner *you* that is always there?

––––––––––––

Three years and two little girls later, I finally finished the journal I started during my first pregnancy. Here is my last entry in that same journal:

> *A funky feeling has come over me, and I know it's because I haven't been able to clear my mind for weeks. It seems that I've come to rely on this journal as a form of therapy, a way to touch a wiser part of myself or the universe, a way to put things back in order. This journal is almost full, and what a different woman I am now than I was when I started it. At the first entry, I was six weeks pregnant with my first child. Now, three years later, there are two beautiful girls snuggled up in our bed next to their father.*
>
> *Everyone should keep a journal in order to see the amazing growth that occurs in a person's life. If it's not written down, not*

captured in some way, it could just slip by, unnoticed . . . another year, another day, another precious moment.

Sandy, you can do anything. Write books and songs, raise children and gardens, be happy, and be grateful. Love and live compassionately. You are a better person than when you started this book; be proud of who you have become.

Unexpected Transitions

Usually we go through huge personal growth during times of transition and change. Because we are creatures of comfort, sometimes that growth feels forced upon us. Every time we grow, we must examine our self-image and reimagine how our lives could be. Ideally, we will embrace the process of learning and expanding. If we can look at these transitions as ongoing occurrences, and view ourselves as changing a little every day, then the process will feel more natural. Many people describe this as finding their "new normal." Some changes are bigger than others, but each day we change and grow; as we age, we gain knowledge and wisdom.

Your journal can be the open window through which your wisdom illuminates your life. Use your journal to reflect on how changes are affecting your life and how you can use these transitions as opportunities to grow, enjoy your life, and achieve the highest vision you have for yourself.

In his book *What Happy People Know*, Dan Baker, PhD, suggests, "Life hurts. If it doesn't hurt some of the time, it's not life. But you can't allow yourself to get wrapped up in

this hurt, constantly reliving it, fearing the future and griev-
ing the past."[2]

Maybe your primary relationship is on the rocks or there
has been a death or serious illness in your family. You may
believe that these tough times are not the best times to keep
notes. However, the act of writing can bring you home again,
back to your true self. Life can get confusing on occasion. It's
easy to feel out of control. If you notice yourself wondering,
"What am I doing? I feel so confused," consider that your
journal may hold some answers for you.

The biggest life transitions usually involve changes on
both the outside and the inside. No matter how set in our
ways we may be, a big life transition forces us to look a little
deeper and adjust to new and possibly shifting circumstances. It's a great idea to use your journal to examine how
external changes are shifting your internal world. How do
you feel about this? How would you like to handle things?
Make a plan. How would you like your life to look and feel
on the other side of these transitions?

The following journal entry was written many years ago
by Jamie, a single mother who was ending yet another relationship:

*So, here I sit with tear-stained sheets. I write it out so that I can
sleep. I tell myself, PLEASE not again, so scared, a heart can
never mend.*

> *Don't look!*
> *Don't fall!*
> *Don't love!*
> *Don't give!*

It hurts! God! It hurts.

My mind whirls around with old clichés: "It's better to have loved and lost..." Is it? My optimism argues with my pessimism. Somewhere there's "a hell-of-a-man" who wants "a hell-of-a-woman" like me. No one will ever want the responsibility of three kids. I have soooo much to offer, soooo much love bottled up inside to give! A modern man doesn't want a dependent (housewife) woman. An old-fashioned man sees me as much too independent for him.

Why, why, oh why does love hurt? These knots in my stomach play tug-of-war with the knots in my throat.

Damn you! Why can't you see... don't you see what you're losing?? Why can't I rid myself of these feelings of loneliness, of needing someone? What have I ever done to deserve this? NOTHING!

So God has something better in mind for me. But when, God, when? I try to be patient, but it's so hard!

Tears, tears, tears.

Like a pressure valve, they finally bring relief.

Down, down, down I go.

I have a feeling of drowning — of reaching out for you, but your indifference does not save me. When I reach the bottom of the well, there's only one way to go: pick myself up, brush myself off, and start all over again. Maybe I loved you more than I've ever loved, but I have confidence in me. I know that, once I make up my mind, I can do anything I make up my mind to do!

If you are going through a particularly difficult experience, you will definitely want to use your journal to help you work through it. Your journal is your calm oasis in the center of the storm. No matter what may be swirling around you, you can use it as a tool to create peace. You may have to dump some of the whipping winds and driving rain onto the page in order to find the calm, but it is there.

Today Jamie has been married for over six years to a man she describes as "the most kind, gentle, compassionate man" she's ever known. She's now grateful that the relationship she described in her journal ended. His selfishness permeated their relationship, and she knows she would have never been truly happy with him. Jamie's children are now grown, and she is a grandmother. She and her husband are spending their retirement traveling and enjoying life.

Try This

The Other Side of the Mountain

Picture this transition in your life as a mountain. You are hiking upward. The terrain is steep and sometimes slippery. You may feel out of breath, exhausted, like you need to take a break. Here it is: your break, your journal. Look around for the guideposts. Guideposts are signs along the path of your life that show how far you've traveled and what direction you're headed in; they often give you clues as to where to go next. A guidepost could be a major change you've experienced that has brought about new beginnings and possibilities. It could be a life event that has defined who you are today.

Imagine gathering your strength and finally reaching the top of this mountain. The air is clean and crisp. Take a deep breath. Look out into the distance and survey the endless possibilities. Write about how it feels to be standing on top of this "mountain," this change you're going through. The hard climb is behind you. You can relax and enjoy the view. How would you like your life to look on the other side of this transition? Write about some of these possibilities.

Recycle into Clarity

Whatever you are feeling, your journal will soak it up and recycle it into something useful. It may not be directly apparent how this writing will be of use to you in your life, but hang in there. All will be revealed. Many times, I've gone to my journal in hopes of just clearing out some negativity that seems to be saturating my life, and then, magically, I get lost in the act of writing. Voilà! A transformation appears on the page. Many times I can't even remember what I've written. I only know that I feel better. When I look back and read what came out, I am often amazed at what showed up. For example:

> *I feel like I'm just barely holding on. I could lose it at any moment. It would be so easy to step across that line into insanity. A tiny thread that is already frayed is tying me to this world. Haley is fourteen months old, and I'm six months pregnant with our second child. I have no moments to myself. I've been yelling a lot the last few days. I don't know how to handle this; I'm not feeling like a good mom. I'm out of touch with what Haley wants and needs, and with what I need. I don't know if I can*

give her what she needs; I feel like there is nothing left. All of the good emotions have been used up and only the bad, mean, angry ones are left.

I think I need to make an effort for myself — maybe set my alarm earlier and meditate or read... do something for me. Fill myself up with good energy for the day. I don't like how I feel, as though I don't have anything inside for Haley. How am I gonna do it for two?

The magnificent souls who attend my journaling workshops have taught me that lots of people feel they're "barely holding on" at one time or another. During this time in my life, I felt as if I was the only person in the world who experienced these feelings, and my journal was the place I could turn when life overwhelmed me. The wonderful thing about writing down my troubles was that, after I dumped my emotions on the paper, answers came from somewhere: "I think I need to make an effort for myself — maybe set my alarm earlier and meditate or read... Do something for me. Fill myself up with good energy for the day." I am always amazed at the wisdom that exists inside each of us.

It may take a while to apply the counsel of your inner wisdom to your daily life; it certainly did for me. We usually don't understand how badly we need to take time away from responsibilities and fill ourselves up again. Although the answers were coming through on the page as I journaled, it took a few sessions for me to heed my own inner wisdom. Then I realized that waking up before my family to meditate, journal, or read affected my entire being. Even in those sleep-deprived years of having little babies, a few moments of quiet contemplation filled me up much more than shut-eye ever could.

It is often difficult to sneak out of bed without waking a nursing toddler or other family members, but if that's the only time you have for journaling, you'll find it's worth the effort. When you go to your journal with a problem or a yucky feeling, after a few minutes or a few pages a wonderful shift can occur. Your drama and negativity can be transformed into clarity. The peacefulness will return, and you will eventually feel okay again. You may even have a revelation!

Those are the moments that keep you coming back to your journal. I can't guarantee that you'll have big breakthroughs every time you write. But I can promise that if you give yourself fully to the practice of journaling, and you continue to use techniques such as dumping, dialoguing, and recycling your emotions into clarity, you will feel the shifts.

Now that you've made some progress with the inner demons, it's time to tackle the ones that live next door. In the next chapter, we will discuss our human mirrors — the people who bring out our beauty and bring up our stuff, and how they help us on the path to becoming who we were meant to be.

CHAPTER 5

Mirror, Mirror
on the Wall

M any years ago, I heard an analogy about oranges and people that really made sense. When you squeeze an orange, what comes out? Orange juice. Why? Because that's what's inside. It's the same with people. It doesn't matter who or what is squeezing us; it could be a mother-in-law, someone who cuts us off in traffic, a boss, or a bill collector. If anger, jealousy, and pain are coming out of you, it's because that's what's inside. The world is just holding up a mirror to let you see what you feel inside. If we fill ourselves with love, joy, and compassion, we will begin to experience more of those qualities in our lives, no matter how hard we're being squeezed.

If we are feeling a little rushed, we will probably find ourselves faced with frequent red lights during our daily commute. If we've made a declaration to avoid sugar, everywhere we turn people will be offering us cakes, cookies, and homemade brownies. Whatever we are internally consumed with — good or bad, terrible or wonderful — it is going to show up around us sooner or later. Until we feel peace inside ourselves, red lights and sugar pushers are going to be out there to put on the pressure.

Your journal is a terrific place to explore letting go of consuming feelings and thoughts about whatever or whoever is squeezing you. You can use journaling to eliminate negativity and make room for positive images and qualities. As you fill yourself with better stuff, that's what you will begin to see reflected in the world around you.

Relationships Are Mirrors

Every day, our relationships show us what we're holding inside and who we are at our best and our worst. Sometimes these are things we'd rather not see. Certain people come into our lives — family, friends, bosses, and neighbors — who have a way of bringing up our issues.

You know the feeling: You're going blissfully through your day, humming a happy tune, and then someone shows up at your doorstep or calls you on the phone and, with one little remark or a glance in your direction, this person whips you into a frenzy. Afterward, your overanalyzing mind kicks in and you find yourself going over every detail of the interaction and getting angry, scared, or insecure.

Whatever emotion comes up, it is strong; it feels uncontrollable and instinctual. Most of the time, these reactions point to parts of ourselves that we have yet to accept. For example, when Aunt Edna suggests we skip that extra piece of cheesecake, why do we feel so defensive? Perhaps she is there to reflect our own shortage of self-love and acceptance; she is shining a light on a feeling of inadequacy or self-judgment that we are burying deep inside. We choose teachers like Aunt Edna because they are exactly what we need to stretch us past our self-imposed limitations. They act as mirrors, reflecting something within ourselves that we have yet to come to terms with. These encounters are arranged by the universe, and they almost always present an opportunity for growth.

Can you think of a person who acts as a mirror in your life? Once you've picked a person or a situation, it's usually easy to figure out what this mirror is there to teach you. You only have to step away from the emotions long enough to view the relationship from a different perspective. Your journal is the perfect place to gain this perspective.

I've had many teachers in my life, but none as influential as my two daughters. Just when I was beginning to feel like I had a few things figured out about my life and my identity, these two little people came along to test me twenty-four hours a day. They ensure that I'm constantly grounded in who I am. Sometimes they reflect light and joy. Other times, chaos and madness come back to me.

For instance, as I write this chapter, my six- and seven-year-old daughters are both home from school with strep throat. Although I've barely worked this week, if I tell them I can't lie in bed and watch a movie, play a game, or read a book, they know exactly what to say that will absolutely maximize my guilt. "You *never* play with us anymore. You care more about your book than us." My personal favorite is, "Mom, all we ever hear about is journalution, journalution, journalution!" They are serving to mirror my guilty feelings about spending time focused on anything that isn't directly related to them.

Balancing our needs against the needs of others is a common dilemma. But our internal response to such situations is what's interesting. My rational mind tells me what a good example I'm setting for my daughters by following my passion and attempting to contribute something positive to the world. After all, one day they will be grown women, too, and I want them to have passionate, fulfilling lives. However, another voice inside warns that they will be all grown up in the blink of an eye, so I must give them all the love I can, immediately. I believe this guilty voice comes from a little girl (me) whose mother was forced to work extremely long hours. That little girl yells at me for putting anything ahead of my daughters. Do you struggle with placing your needs above other demands on your time? Can you trace your feelings to something deeper in your past?

Potentially, everyone you meet is a mirror for you. It could be the guy at the grocery store or the woman who does your dry cleaning. It doesn't matter. Mirrors are everywhere. What is being reflected to you today? Are you seeing smiling faces and hearing laughter? Or are you seeing grimaces and and hearing people complaining under their breath? Or, even worse, are negative comments being thrown your way? Does it feel like everyone is out to get you today? I challenge you to use your journal to make the most of the human mirrors you meet out in the world. Ask yourself about the reflections you are seeing. What meaning could you extract from these human mirrors?

Intimate Relationships

Our most meaningful relationships are the intimate ones. When you are in a relationship that is troubling, or that brings up volatile emotions, it is a great opportunity to look at what it might be mirroring to you and ask yourself how to learn from it.

Here is a journal entry from Jade, as she works through a breakup with yet another man:

I saw him. I was at dinner with Megan and, from across the room, I saw him. Josh, sitting there with another beautiful girl. My heart pounded so loud in my head, I felt cold and hot at the same time. I prayed he wouldn't see me, and then I prayed he would. I tried to ignore them, but I couldn't help myself. I stared

at her. She looked so innocent. And I had a revelation: I've
changed. I would never allow myself to be in a relationship like
that again. I would never stand for the bull-$#@! that I put up
with from him. I wouldn't take him back if he came crawling on
his hands and knees (although that might be fun to watch)!

After all the struggles, the anger, the hurt,
The result was relief!
I saw him for the first time in six months.
I saw his face.
I saw the eyes that looked for ways to betray me.
I saw the mouth that told the lies.
I saw the smile that deceived me.
And then I saw his next victim,
And I thanked God that it was no longer me.

All the relationships we have, and especially the intimate
ones, demonstrate something about our inner esteem, even
if it's only how well or poorly we stand up for ourselves, or
how we teach others to treat us in every moment and interaction. Jade told me that, through the act of journaling, she
was able to see the mirror her boyfriend had been during
their relationship. By taking advantage of Jade's open heart
and her insecurities, he showed her that she was not valuing
herself. Subconsciously, she was probably attracted to him
in the first place because he validated her own poor self-
image. She also realized that he would probably never
change, and that it doesn't necessarily make him a terrible
person. She had *allowed* him to treat her poorly. By journaling about accidentally running into her ex-boyfriend and all

of the emotions that came up for her, she realized that she no longer wanted to be in a dishonest relationship.

Jade is in a healthier place in her life now; she spends less time worrying about what her boyfriends think and more time pursuing her own joy. Jade was able to see what her life would have been like if she'd stayed in a relationship with this man, and she was grateful to have grown and moved on.

Try This
Mirror, Mirror on the Wall

Here's a good place to start. Think of the last time you were mad at someone close to you. Or if anger isn't your biggest issue, think of someone who hurt you, broke your heart, or betrayed your trust. Recall in vivid detail what made you so upset. Write the situation down in your journal. Take as much time as you need to capture the details on the page.

After you've written out the scenario, make a quick list of words or phrases that describe the other person in this situation (e.g., selfish, controlling, heartless). Write at least three words. Then ask yourself if you've ever displayed the same characteristics or said similar things. While your first response may be "No! Of course not!" look a little deeper. Is there anyone on the planet who might remember a moment when you have behaved in that way? Write about that now.

Stepping back from your position and viewing a mirroring relationship in your journal can help you gather lessons for your life path. Ask yourself, "What is this person here to teach me?" Eventually, you may even come to view this relationship as a blessing that leads to a greater understanding about your life.

A Lesson from One of My Mirrors

Many years ago, I received a valuable lesson from one of my mirrors. John, a dear friend of mine, was dating a woman I did not like. At the time, I felt justified in my disapproval of his relationship, and I did little to hide it. I frequently bombarded him with my opinions about why the relationship was not in his best interest. When I was alone, I found myself obsessing over how his life was turning out and questioning what made him want to put himself in this situation. Hours after being with him, I would review our conversations in my head and analyze his comments and motivations. I can't begin to estimate the amount of time I spent obsessing about my friend's life.

Then, thanks to journaling, I had a revelation. I had just returned from another uncomfortable evening with John and his girlfriend, Sue. I was spewing on and on in my journal about his life and his relationship. I could feel the negativity pouring out of me, and for just a moment I saw myself from a distance, as if I were floating. I heard a voice ask, "Is this the kind of energy you want to put out in the world?" I grimaced with disgust at my conduct. I wrote, "This is not who I want to be. I want to be filled with love and compassion. I don't want to be consumed with negativity all the time." I had a vision that life is like a garden, and I was so busy worrying about my friend's garden that there were now weeds and dead flowers all around mine. I was working at a job that I despised. I was pregnant with my first child and refused to look at the insecurities this was bringing up in my life and my marriage. I had plenty of work to do on my own life, but I had been too obsessed with John's life to even notice.

Can any part of you relate to this? Have you ever appointed yourself chief landscaper in someone else's garden? You may love tomatoes and your neighbor may plant broccoli. You can probably think of all kinds of reasons why tomatoes are much better than broccoli. However, that doesn't make tomatoes right and broccoli wrong. It's just another choice. Tending your own garden is a big job, and it requires constant attention; you really don't have time to be taking care of other people's gardens, even if they ask you to. You must focus your energy on your own life. And when you do so, amazing, beautiful things will begin to grow.

During that journaling session, I decided that I was going to give up worrying about my friend's life and instead cultivate love and kindness in my own. I made a decision to let it go. It was a wonderful feeling of release. As I relinquished my imaginary hold on my friend's relationship, relief flooded my body. I also asked for help from the Divine energy of the universe in learning to *love* John's girlfriend — the same woman I'd wasted so much time fighting against.

At that moment, loving Sue seemed like a far-fetched, out-rageous goal. But I asked for help anyway.

Months later, my first daughter was born. After her birth, a new relationship blossomed between Sue and me. She was great with my baby, she understood my style of mothering, and my daughter loved her. As a result, Sue became the one person I trusted with my children, and I felt more and more love for her each time I was with her. The outrageous request I had made in my journal had been magically granted.

The lesson this particular human mirror brought into my life was about judgment and surrender. I had been judging Sue and her relationship with my friend. I discovered that I was focusing all my energy on John's life because it was easier to try to fix him than to look at my own life.

Surrendering your need to judge other people's lives will free energy in you to concentrate on what you want to create in your own life and in the world. If I had not recognized this lesson, it would probably have been mirrored back to me through other relationships. Doesn't it seem wasteful to spend time worrying about someone else's life when there's so much you can do with your own?

Access the Power You Find in the Mirror

One of the common themes I've discovered among avid journalers is that, as they begin to access their own power, they search for ways to contribute to the world on a grander scale. The daily dramas that have monopolized their existence in the past begin to fade as their lives take on a grander vision.

Rhonda, a thirty-year-old mom, started a mother's support group with her friend Tanya. She used her writing to determine what this mirroring relationship was teaching her then went on to use her newfound power to help others. Here is her journal entry:

> *I was so excited about our support group meeting on Saturday. Then Tanya called tonight and said she didn't want Robert (my thirteen-month-old son) to be there. It was a difficult conversation. All of my insecurities came up — feeling left out, excluded from the group. So now I'm trying to figure this out. I can't sleep. This has been the theme of the last two weeks. First, having to skip the wedding (because my son was not invited), and now this. Me having to make tough decisions in order to "walk my talk."*
>
> *If we don't make the choice or the arrangements to include our children in our lives, then who will? How can I ever expect women to be able to take their children to work or to luncheons, how can I ever expect children to be welcomed everywhere when my own mothering friends are not willing to welcome them into our little group or to their weddings? It's strange, but I feel pretty calm. I feel that this is what I am all about . . . this is my life's message or purpose.*
>
> *I want to learn from this. What is this teaching me, what issues is it bringing up?*
>
> *Definitely the insecurity thing. That first moment when I hung up the phone with Tanya, it felt like I was back in the fifth grade trying to be included in the popular group. I could*

only envision everybody being there except me — me being
left out.

    But now I feel okay with that. I know I'm being true to
myself. That's what I hope to teach my children to do, right from
the start, and not give in to peer pressure just to be "in."

    I keep having this knot in my stomach, telling me that my
friendship with Tanya is going down the tubes. She brings up all
of my insecurities about being left out, not liked, cut off from the
"in" group. But I know deep down that my path is not about
being included. I think I am learning to separate from the gang
and follow my own path. Just keep doing what you're doing.

Rhonda told me that her friendship with Tanya has
changed since she wrote this entry in her journal. They still
speak, but Rhonda realized that it is no longer a priority for
her to have a large number of friends or events to attend.
She has begun to look at her life through a larger lens, and
to focus on how she can contribute to the world in a positive way. One way in which she expresses her passion is by
working with corporations to develop on-site day care facil-
ities, so that parents can be close to their young children if
staying at home is not an option. Rhonda told me that her
journal was a friend and companion to her while she worked
through these lessons and grew to be more confident in herself and her journey.

    When you begin to use your human mirrors as a tool for
growth, rather than allowing yourself to create drama in
your life, you will feel a renewed sense of energy. You will be
able to use this energy to contribute to the good in the

world, which will, in turn, supply you with even more energy and enthusiasm for life.

Here's an exercise to help you access your own inner power:

Try This
What's Your Big Picture?

Imagine that all the people and situations that have caused you grief in the past have been magically transformed and understood as life lessons. They no longer take energy from you each day. Your slate is clean, and you are ready to make your contribution to the world. Take a deep breath. Create a vision of yourself that encompasses the greatest dream you can hold for your life. Imagine that nothing is off limits, and you are ready to live a *big* life. What could this be? What is the whisper that gives you butterflies in your belly? Write it down. Exhale the fear and allow your vision to flow onto the page. You don't have to worry about how to accomplish it right now; you must only capture the dream on the page. If you have several outrageous visions, write them all down. Let your dreams marinate in your journal for a while.

Look Beyond the Superficial

How many times have you been forced to spend a few awkward moments with a complete stranger? It happens all the time on public transportation, in elevators, and standing in line at the grocery store. Do those moments leave you feeling enriched, or empty? Can you imagine being a mirror for joy and bliss in your world?

In the book *Riding the Bus with My Sister,* author Rachel Simon describes her initial skepticism that a bus driver who studied archaeology and photography in college could be truly fulfilled by just driving a city bus. After many conversations with passengers, the driver turned to Rachel and said, "See, it's not the driving. I spend my day meeting people...And that's what I like about it. There's so much richness on a bus — really, so much richness everywhere — if you just develop the ability to look at life with a different eye, and appreciate the opportunities offered to you."[1]

So how can you develop this ability to connect with the richness inside everybody you meet? All you have to do is use your journal to look a little deeper. It's easy to just go through the motions, barely interacting with another human being all day, having only superficial conversations when absolutely necessary. It does take a little stretching of your comfort zone to connect with the people around you. It requires looking into the eyes of your coworker and listening intently to her answer when you say, "Hello, how are you?"

At first, it may feel uncomfortable to strike up a conversation in the elevator when it's so easy to stare at the floor and wait for your destination. However, you will find that a tiny effort on your part to brighten someone else's day can have a huge effect on your life, too. You may just find that the world magically becomes a friendlier place, and wonderful opportunities and events seem to fall into your lap out of the clear blue sky.

Recording your observations about people in a journal is a wonderful way to develop your ability to look at life with a different eye. There is richness everywhere. You only need to train yourself to see it, and the world will reflect your internal abundance.

Try This
Reflecting and Connecting

Recall the last person you stood face-to-face with today. What was the overall feeling of energy you exchanged with this person? Remember the exact conversation and summarize it in your journal. Now take that interaction and imagine how you could have made it even better. If the interaction was friendly, could you have taken it to a deeper level by looking directly into the person's eyes and asking about his or her day? If it was someone you spend a lot of time with (a family member, partner, or coworker), were you really paying attention to the interaction, or were you trying to do fifty things at once? Write down an improved version of the interaction.

Tomorrow, I challenge you to make an effort to change the conversation you normally have with the mailman or the woman in the elevator. Give a little more of yourself in the way you say hello, look that person directly in the eyes, try feeling and reflecting love behind your eyes before you begin a conversation, and notice the difference it makes in your day. If you actually take the time to breathe a loving breath into your next conversation, or even your next smile at a stranger, it will have a gigantic effect on your life. Try it!

Rediscover Your Inner Dreamer

Inside every person on this planet, there is an inner dreamer. In order to mirror a sense of joy on a daily basis, it helps to be completely connected with your inner dreamer. This isn't about the dreams you have while sleeping, but the dreams you hold deep in your heart about the world and what you'd like to be. It's the little person most of us lost touch with when we were children, usually between the ages of six and sixteen. Often, we lose touch with our inner dreamer when something traumatic happens and we realize that life is not all fun and games. Your event could have been a harsh criticism of a painting or song you created, or it could have been the way your father looked at you when you struck out in the Little League playoffs. Whatever it was, when it occurred a small part of you began to shut down.

As children, we express every emotion we have as soon as we feel it. If something tastes bad, we spit it out; if we are excited about something, we dance and sing and jump around. But as we grow up, we are taught that it's not always appropriate to express our emotions. We learn that it might hurt Aunt Sally's feelings if we spit out her homemade split-pea soup at the table, or that it would crush Great

Uncle Bob if we ran from the room screaming "Peeee-eeewwwww!" after a cigar-scented hug. Or our parents say, "Big boys don't cry." So we begin to stifle our emotions. We stuff them down and, if we don't release them, they stay stuck deep inside, forgotten but not always benign. The earnest child we once were gets replaced by an adult with suppressed emotions and lost ideals. There lies the inner dreamer. Sometimes lost and confused, sometimes lonely and bored, that inner dreamer has been waiting for years to be recognized and invited back out to play.

If you have trouble figuring out what you want to do with your life, your inner dreamer holds the key. If you are still looking for Mr. or Ms. Right, your inner dreamer can be your guide. Although it can take practice to look deeply inside and see the inner dreamer in ourselves or in an unfriendly, angry person, he or she is always there. Just taking an extra moment to acknowledge your inner dreamer in your journal can make all the difference in how you feel today.

Here is an early journal entry in which I attempted to connect with the little girl inside me and start an ongoing conversation:

Dear Sandy,

I lost you when I was seven years old. I abandoned you just like he did. I miss you. I can't remember what made you laugh, what made you special. Hello? Are you in there? It's okay to come out now. Can you come out and talk to me?

Yes, but I'm scared.

What are you afraid of?
I'm not sure.
I'll be strong for you. I'm here to take care of you now. It's
going to be okay.

At that point in my life, I was so out of touch with
myself that I had to begin by slowly uncovering the little girl
first. Gradually, I felt her presence more. She began to share
her dreams and visions in my journals. These were dreams
that I had lost or buried long ago. The joy crept back into
my life as the anger and pain drained from my fingertips
onto the page.

Can you think of any dreams you've given up along the
way? Begin to use your journal to reconnect to the visions
you held for yourself when you were young. Your journal
will remind you to view the world from your inner dreamer's
perspective and to incorporate things into your life every day
that will make her smile.

Try This

Conversation with Your Inner Dreamer

Now it's your turn to begin a conversation with your inner
dreamer. This is a fun exercise that will help you remember
all the wonderful qualities you possessed as a child and get
back in touch with some of those free-spirited character
traits.

Visualize your early childhood. What are some of the

memories that stand out? Were you a happy child? What made you happiest? What troubled you? Write a letter to yourself as a child. Ask a few questions of your inner dreamer and write the first responses that pop into your mind. If you're having difficulty connecting to your inner dreamer, try writing the questions with your dominant hand and the answers with the other hand. Write as a child would write.

Seeing the Inner Dreamer in Others

Inside, we are all just little children trying to heal, trying to do the best we can in this world. Many times it doesn't look like that to others, though. Often, the child inside is angry and resentful; it may even want to hurt others. When someone else's inner dreamer is having a meltdown, your journaling and healing processes can be especially valuable to you. You have no control over how another person reacts to you or what they say and do, but you always have control over your reaction. However, you may not always *feel* like you have control; sometimes emotions take over, and it seems like you can't stop them. When this happens, your journal can be the best place to dump your emotions, gain clarity, and begin again.

When you are in conflict with someone, no matter what you are feeling in any moment, try to remember that there is a wounded child inside the other person, too. Underneath it all, what people really want and need is human connection.

You could be the one to make a difference in that person's life. I ask you to respond to the other person with love. I am calling on you to be one of the souls who stands up for loving-kindness, compassion, and connection. You are being asked to take the first step and unite with other human beings, rather than responding to anger with more anger, and hate with more hate. Use your journal to practice connecting to the inner dreamer in yourself and others with kindness and compassion, especially if others provide difficult mirrors for you. Take the insights and revelations that come from your journaling practice out into the world!

Try This
Spread the Love

Take your journal to a public park, mall, or bookstore. Choose a place to sit where you can observe many people of different ages. Spend a few moments just watching everyone. Notice the differences and the similarities. See if you can get a feeling about various people's lives based on what they are wearing, the way they walk, or what they are doing. Compare the way adults carry themselves to the way the children interact. Try smiling at strangers. Do you get different reactions from grown-ups and children? Is it difficult to make eye contact with people?

Make some notes about your initial impressions of your fellow human beings. Allow compassion to fill your body, and let yourself imagine how you might contribute some positive energy to the public space. Could you strike up a conversation with an elderly person? Could you make a sign that says "Smile!" and hang it where many people will see it? Write down a few ideas about how you can contribute some good vibes to the world.

_____

Seek Wisdom from a Master

Connecting to the best in others isn't always easy. However, it is worth the effort to look for ways to rise above pettiness and attempt to learn from all of our human mirrors. During one particularly difficult relationship, I used the Dalai Lama as my role model. At the time, I was reading his book, *The Art of Happiness.*[2] When it felt as if my emotions were getting the best of me, I would visualize the Dalai Lama sitting in front of me. I could see his kind eyes and laughing energy emanating from his body. I would ask him what he would do and how he would react in my situation. Every time I did this, I felt wiser and more compassionate.

Try This
Meet the Masters

Choose anyone, alive or dead, who you view as enlightened. It could be Mother Mary, Jesus, Buddha, or the angel of your grandmother. It doesn't matter. The goal is to tap into this person's wisdom and compassion. Begin by sitting comfortably with your journal in your lap. Close your eyes and visualize your enlightened guide across from you. Imagine what the person is wearing, how he or she would smell, and every detail of his or her face. Look deeply into the wise one's eyes and ask for guidance. How would your wise guide handle the person or situation you're dealing with? Now open your eyes and write down any feelings or visions that pop into your mind.

Next, ask your guide to accompany you in your future interactions with others. Visualize your guide becoming transparent. Take a deep breath, inhaling the essence of this wise soul. See misty vapors surrounding your body like a fog, and imagine your body absorbing your guide's essence. Pick up your pen, and write in your journal as if you *are* your guide. Imagine your next encounter with a difficult person or situation. The difference is that now your guide inhabits your body. This may seem silly, but try it! Your mind is extremely powerful, so using this visualization can give you courage and compassion beyond your wildest imagination.

As I mentioned in the introduction, if you are reading this book, you have been called to add your light and love to the world. This is the part of your journey where you will begin to feel your passion for life. Journaling will assist you in discovering your purpose. As you touch others' lives, *your* life will be transformed. The human mirrors that give us the most trouble are really gifts of healing and transformation. Once you are able to use these situations and relationships to practice your wisdom, you will be a beacon of light on the planet. You will be able to use this new energy to live a life of joy and compassion — even bliss.

So far, we have looked at how to view your life from a higher perspective and use your relationships as a tool for discovering your inner wisdom. Let's take it a step further by capturing your wishes in a journal and asking the universe to take part in manifesting a life that is joyful, inspiring, and fulfilling. In the next chapter, we will begin the process of using your journal to mastermind alliances and manifest your deepest dreams.

CHAPTER 6

Hopes, Dreams, and Visions

Remember the scene in *The Wizard of Oz* when Dorothy asks Glenda the Good Witch how to get back to Kansas? Glenda tells Dorothy, "My dear, you've always had the power." We all have the power to create a life we love. But often, like Dorothy, we look in faraway places for our answers when the real answers are in our own backyard. It's tempting to look outside ourselves for answers to life's big questions. After all, if we could just read a book or go to a seminar and discover our true purpose, it would make things so much easier. While the answers that others have found may inspire you, ultimately you have to answer life's big questions for yourself, and your journal is the perfect place to begin figuring out your hopes, dreams, and visions. Think of your journal as your very own pair of ruby slippers.

We've examined how to use your journal to put people and situations in a context that will help you heal your wounds and extract meaning and purpose from your life. In this chapter, I encourage you to take another step and put your deepest hopes and dreams down on the paper. Use your journal to allow the universe to help you manifest a life that is exciting, fulfilling, and rewarding — one that makes you want to jump out of bed in the morning because you are so excited to be alive. We've all experienced moments of Divine inspiration, when nothing feels out of reach; the world is our oyster and we've got it all figured out. Your journal is the perfect place for creating more of these Divinely inspired moments. This chapter will help you capture your dreams and visions, then develop a plan to make them come true.

What Do You Really Want?

In my workshops, I often ask, "If I had a magic wand and I could grant you anything, could you tell me what you truly wanted?" Many times, I see panic on the faces of the participants; although they may have an idea of what they'd like, it's difficult for them to put it into words. Ask yourself now: Do you really know what you want? If you had to state your greatest desire out loud, in a succinct, passionate sentence, could you do it?

Have you ever made a list of things you'd like to create in your life? This is a fun exercise that starts with simply listing all the things you love. When you focus on what you love, you can begin to manifest it gradually, day by day. As you become more in tune with the things that make your life special, your passion and purpose will rise to the surface in your daily life.

Try This
Things I Love

Write the prompt "Things I Love" at the top of a new page in your journal. Take a deep breath, then focus on keeping your pen moving for at least five minutes. Make a list of things that bring you joy. Include items that cost a lot of money, as well as things that are free: the smell of freshly brewed coffee in the morning, watching the ocean, the feel of sand under your bare feet, bubble baths, pedicures, vacations, rainbows, thunderstorms, snowflakes, football games, chocolate, giggles. The list should contain the big and little things in life that make you smile.

Copy this list onto the inside cover of your journal. Add to it whenever you remember or discover something else that fills you up with good energy. Review your list each week and pick one thing to give to yourself, whether it's a long walk in the woods or splurging on a massage.

Look for ways to make your day wonderful today. Give yourself a big hug by celebrating some of these things that bring you joy and make you unique. Enjoy your "Things I

Love" list and add to it often. Share it with a friend or loved one on your next birthday.

A Vision

Having a vision for your life inspires you and guides you every day in all your actions. It gives your life meaning and purpose. It's easy to just go through the motions, checking things off your to-do list and never looking up long enough to ask, "Is this what I really want?" Having a written vision for your life keeps you on track. When distractions come up or you have to make tough decisions, it can help to go back and look at the vision you created, reminding yourself of what you truly want. Then you can ask yourself if this next step or decision is in line with your greater vision for your life. So take a moment and answer this question in your journal: Is this what you really want your life to look like?

Try This

Is This What You Really Want?

Write the question "Is this what I really want?" at the top of a blank page in your journal. Then close your eyes and take three deep breaths. Now write for ten minutes. Write about all the wonderful things you have in your life. Write about all the things you may have forgotten you wanted. Write about the things you let go of because they seemed too difficult or too time-intensive or financially impossible. Let yourself write what you really, really want. Don't edit anything; allow your thoughts to flow onto the page. If you envision yourself as a lawyer fighting for children's rights and you haven't completed high school, don't worry; just write it down. This is not the time to critique your dreams but to get your desires down on the page. No one ever has to read this. Whatever the critic inside your head is saying to you, release it and surrender it. Keep writing your deepest dreams and desires, and soon the critical voice will fade into the background. As you write your dreams, you give them wings. They will float off the page and conspire with the universe to bring you the life you really want.

How did that feel? Did anything surprising show up on the page? Did you feel hopeless that you'll never have what you really want, or did you feel excited about rediscovering something you lost? It really doesn't matter; just remember that any emotions that come up for you can all be worked out on the blank page. Writing in your journal about what you really want will automatically attract circumstances that can arrange for those exact things to happen. That is why you must be very clear. They say "Be careful what you wish for, because you just might get it." To some degree this is true, but in a good way; as these things you've always wanted begin to appear, you may realize that some are not so important to you after all. Your vision will begin to shift and develop into what you truly desire. In fact, your vision may change dramatically over time, so it is a good idea to consistently re-create and revise your vision in your journal. If you do so, it will always reflect what you want to attract.

Actress Salma Hayek has talked about how she wished to be a famous actress, but as she achieved success in her own country as a beloved soap opera star, she questioned whether that role was the right thing for her. Later, when she became a successful actress in Hollywood (which everyone told her she was crazy to attempt, barely speaking English at the time), she again questioned whether the dream she had achieved was what she truly wanted. Finally, she realized that her dream was not just to be a famous actress, but to contribute something she was proud of — something that would be a lasting symbol of her voice in the world. She explained how she figured this out for herself: "How do you recognize what is your true dream and what is the dream that you are dreaming for other people to love you? If you enjoy the process, it's your dream. If you are enduring the process, just desperate for the result, it's somebody else's dream."[1] Use your journal to make certain that the work you are doing and the life you are living, every day, in your every action, reflects your true dream, not somebody else's.

Lessons in Manifestation

In 1992, a friend introduced me to the work of the best-selling author and self-empowerment guru Wayne Dyer. Dr. Dyer's ideas — especially the notion of manifesting our dreams — really resonated with me. Eventually, he proved to me that we really can manifest anything. One day, when I was pregnant with our first child, my husband Rich and I were in the car listening to a tape of Wayne Dyer and

Deepak Chopra. Dr. Dyer was telling a story about his wife, Marcelene, who was working on a book about spirituality and childbirth, and how she had given birth to seven children. He described her birthing process as being incredibly peaceful. Apparently, when she gave birth she would go into an altered state of consciousness and "become one" with the experience. At that point in my own pregnancy, about seven months along, I had read every pregnancy and birthing book I could get my hands on, but I was still in a state of complete fear. As Dr. Dyer continued to describe Marcelene on the tape, I said to Rich, "I want Wayne Dyer's wife to help me give birth!" We laughed. It was a joke.

About two weeks later, I received a call from my father-in-law, who had just purchased four tickets for a Wayne Dyer talk. This was completely out of character for him; he had never read or listened to any of Wayne Dyer's material. The night of the event arrived, and as I attempted to make the extra fifty pounds I was carrying look cute, I joked with my husband again: "I want to meet Wayne Dyer, and I want him to tell his wife to help me give birth!"

That evening, I stood in line during intermission, along with approximately three hundred other excited fans, to get a signed copy of Dr. Dyer's latest book. When I finally reached the front of the line, I asked, "Will your wife's book on childbirth be ready in time to help me?" He said that her book wasn't yet finished, but that she was nearby and I should go say hi to her. He added, "She just *loves* pregnant women." I waddled over with my husband and introduced myself to Marcelene Dyer, then told her about my fear of giving birth and asked if she had any words of wisdom for me. She responded, "It is such a pleasure to meet you. I would be happy to help you in any way I can. In fact, *if you would like me to be at the birth, I would consider it an honor."*

My jaw dropped. I stood in silence, completely stunned. I had joked about this ridiculous scenario several times, and now here was Marcelene Dyer offering it to me! I am grateful that my husband stepped in to exchange phone numbers with her, because I was still frozen. I called later that week, and we talked about Marci's childbirth philosophies.

Marcelene Dyer was with me when I gave birth to both of my daughters. My second daughter was born at home in the water, and I labored for two days. Marci stayed with me the entire time. She slept on my couch, held my hand, and talked to me about my strength and power as a woman. She has become a magical mentor in my life, my true soul sister. I am so blessed and grateful to have her as a friend. In fact, Marci was the first person to suggest that I would write my own book, which also seemed absurd to me at the time.

Until the moment when I met Marcelene, nothing that magical had ever happened to me. But it taught me just how powerful our words and thoughts really are. A simple statement, made out loud and with no attachment — "I want Wayne Dyer's wife to help me give birth" — set events and people in motion, unbeknownst to me, to grant my seemingly ridiculous request. By reading Wayne's books, listening to his tapes, and experimenting with his teachings in my own life, I serendipitously attracted an exemplary mother figure in Marci. Now I model my own mothering skills after her. I began to wonder: If my words and thoughts managed to deliver one outrageous request, what else could I manifest?

Apply This to Your Life

The arrival of Wayne and Marci Dyer in my life exemplifies the saying, "When the student is ready, the teacher will appear." Can you recognize any teachers who are presenting themselves to you today? Are you keeping them at bay, or welcoming them into your life?

Imagine that you hold a magic wand that has the power to grant any wish. What is it you truly want? Are you ready to tell me? I remember Wayne Dyer saying something that applies perfectly: "There is good news and bad news. The good news is that whatever you really, really want, you will get. The bad news is that whatever you really, really don't want, you will also get, because that is what you are thinking about all the time."[2]

I challenge you to write a wonderful vision for something you want to create in your life. Call in the perfect teacher to guide you in creating this new life. Use your journal to do this. While journaling is a wonderful tool for working out your issues and problems, examining the details and decisions, the act of creating an inspiring, passionate vision will have the greatest impact on your life.

Try This
Perfect Day

What is your idea of perfection? Journal your perfect day. Pick one scenario, one blissful day, and capture it in your journal. Write it or draw it, using whatever feels right to you — crayons, markers, photos, whatever you like. Begin with waking up in the morning. In your perfect day, do you wake to watch the sunrise, or do you sleep until noon? Are you looking out a window at the ocean or the mountains? Are you sleeping in a high, pillow-top bed with white linens blowing all around you, on a simple Zen-like futon, or in a tent in the forest? What do you eat for breakfast? Do you stroll to a sidewalk café and drink lattes, or is breakfast served in bed? Do you spend your day laughing with close friends and family by a fire, or are you with your favorite book on a secluded beach? Write about the entire day, morning through night, including as many details as possible. You don't have to limit yourself to one perfect day; after you've completed the first one, write another if you're inspired to. You can never have too many perfect days.

In your journals, you can collect visions of how you would like your days to unfold. Reflect on them often. Meditating on these visions and imagining that you are living them will help attract the circumstances to create them. As you get clearer and clearer about your life and your dreams, paths will appear. You may find yourself fielding invitations that are exact manifestations of the perfect days you wrote about.

My friend Debbie told me that when she was in college, she made a list in her journal of the qualities she wanted in a husband. She decided what was most important to her, such as humor, honesty, and compassion, and she meshed these features together to create her perfect man. Shortly after college, she met and married her dream man, the guy with all the qualities she'd been looking for. After more than ten years of marriage and four children, she told me, "He's probably better than what I visualized."

At one of my journaling workshops, I told the group about Debbie's success. Julia, a thirty-five-year-old woman in the workshop, wrote the following manifesting journal entry after hearing Debbie's story:

> *I am so grateful that I have a magnificently delicious lifetime companion who loves and adores me without smothering me. He is kind, caring, and compassionate. He has work he loves, but has plenty of time to take long breaks for relaxation together. His love of travel matches mine perfectly, and we enjoy taking fabulous vacations together. His sense of humor keeps me laughing, and our relationship has enhanced both of our lives while allowing us to remain powerful, passionate individuals as well. His communication skills guide us through the ups and downs of adjusting to coupledom. I love having a life companion who understands me and encourages me to live up to the highest vision I can create for myself. Thank you so much!*

Julia recently told me she's met a man who fits this description perfectly; they have spent countless hours discussing their future dreams and visions with each other. They've also attended three personal development seminars together in beautiful resort locations. Julia's vision is well on its way to being manifested!

Try This
The Manifesting Game

Pick one thing you would love to manifest in your life right now. It could be a new job, a relationship, or even a new car. Write a vision for this thing or experience. First take a deep breath and get yourself centered and calm. Then, from this calm, quiet space, write your vision exactly as you would like it to unfold. Be as descriptive as possible. Imagine how it will feel when you have this thing you want. After you have written your vision clearly, post it in a place where you can read it daily. Close your eyes and smile after you read it each day. Really *see* your vision coming true.

Jokes from the Universe

You may be surprised by the humor in the universe when it comes to manifesting your vision. I have a funny story about that to share with you. In South Florida, where I live, there are free outdoor concerts in the springtime. While my husband and I were at one of these concerts, I noticed the schedule of upcoming artists. The following month, David Cassidy was coming to play. As a little girl, I worshipped David Cassidy. I grew up watching *The Partridge Family* every day, and I had posters of him all over my room. I remember dancing to his music alone in my room and dreaming of him, as millions of little girls did. When I discovered that he would be playing a free concert, I excitedly ran to tell my husband, who did not share my overwhelming enthusiasm for Mr. Cassidy. I put the date on my calendar and began counting down the days.

During this time, our apartment was on the market, so our realtor would come and go, showing it as needed. Two days before the concert, I received a call from our realtor, saying that someone wanted to see the apartment and they would be there in fifteen minutes. I told her it was impossible; I had just gotten home from a weeklong trip, so the house was a disaster and I was exhausted. The realtor interrupted me: "Wait, before you say no, let me tell you who it is — David Cassidy. Do you know who he is?" I squealed like a schoolgirl. "Do I know who he is?! He's coming to my house??!!!"

I opted to spend the next fifteen minutes fixing my hair and makeup rather than straightening the house. David Cassidy spent about five minutes looking around, then left. Upon reflection, I probably should have put my energy into cleaning the house. When my husband came home and I told him what had happened, he said, "Sandy, you really overshot your manifesting powers this time. You didn't realize when you said 'I want to see David Cassidy' that you would actually draw him to our home!"

Who knows the power of words? If you step back and look at your life as a huge creation, what have your thoughts and words created so far? How does your life look as a big picture? Can you see the circumstances that your thoughts and words have brought about? What would you like to create right now?

Try This

The Dinner Party

Here's a fun list to create in your journal, and also a great topic of conversation at your next cocktail party. Who are the top five people you'd like to have dinner with before you die? For now, use people who are still living, although it's fun to create a list of dead celebrities to dine with, too. For this exercise, imagine that you will eventually manifest a dinner or meeting with these people. Think of everyone in the world — musicians, actors, authors, politicians, athletes — who you'd really love to have an intimate conversation with. Start by writing down every name that pops into your mind. Then, as the days go by, narrow down your list and rank the top five.

What would you ask each person? Why are these particular people on your list? Can you determine what these selections reveal about your hopes and dreams? Describe in vivid detail how the evening would unfold: where the dinner takes place, what circumstances brought you together, and the ongoing conversations and budding friendships that might develop.

Share your list with friends and family. Put it out there. You never know...

Masterminding

When you really want to turn up the heat on manifesting your dreams, you will want to add *masterminding* to your journaling practice. Masterminding is an alliance of two or more people working together toward a goal or vision. When you mastermind, you hold a vision for someone else and they do the same for you; you use your combined energy to attract and create your dreams. The power to manifest these dreams is multiplied when you write them in your journal and share them with your mastermind group. Napoleon Hill wrote in 1927, "The 'Master Mind' may be defined as the coordination of knowledge and effort in a spirit of harmony, between two or more people for the attainment of a definite purpose. When a group of individual brains are coordinated and function in harmony, the increased energy created through that alliance becomes available to every individual brain in the group."[3] From ancient times, people have changed the course of history by applying the mastermind principle.

When I began the process of writing a proposal to get this book published, I kept hearing this word *masterminding* in books I was reading and tapes I was listening to. It was a new concept for me, but it sounded like something I wanted to try. I found three other women who were excited and intrigued by the idea of masterminding, and we began to meet every Wednesday at my home. We named ourselves M2M, which stands for Mastermind to Manifest, because our intention is to manifest our dreams together. The number two signifies the energy that is created when two or more people gather together in the spirit of harmony for a greater purpose.

The most wonderful thing about masterminding is how empowering it feels. Our group encouraged and supported me in launching the journalution. We took famous authors to dinner and gathered endorsements for our projects. We made marketing plans and designed websites, flyers, and press releases. We created goals and supported each other, both when we hit bumps and as we accomplished our goals. Every single one of these goals began around my kitchen table with an idea and a written vision of it being realized. The mastermind group has been a catalyst for it all. I've written some guidelines for creating your own mastermind meeting; you can download a copy by going to the journalution website, www.journalution.com.

Laura Duksta, author of the best-selling self-published children's book *I Love You More*,[4] wrote to me:

> *My mastermind group has been a nurturing and supportive environment. There were many times when I wasn't sure how to move forward, or times when I felt I wasn't doing it "right" or well enough. The group helped me plow through where I might have been stopped alone. They have applauded my successes and lifted me up when I've failed. Masterminding has helped me to see the bigger picture while keeping me from getting too far ahead of myself. It has helped me stay enthusiastic about my projects and given me courage to step way beyond my comfort zone onto a much bigger playing field.*

I believe that when you discover the radical and possibly revolutionary change you can create when you mastermind with others, you will harness the power to change the world. Can you imagine groups of people coming together around the world, supporting each other in living their dreams? What amazing things can we accomplish together by masterminding regularly? Now it's your turn to use masterminding to create the life of your dreams.

Try This
Mastermind

Identify a friend or colleague who is interested in master-minding with you. Ask your friend what one thing he or she would like to have happen: a new job, relationship, home, or whatever. Invite this friend to write an affirmative sentence that expresses gratitude for the fulfillment of that dream. Then write your friend's sentence in your journal.

For example: Emily wants a new career, but she's not sure what she wants to do. Emily writes: "I am so happy to have work that is emotionally and financially rewarding, fun, inspiring, and helpful to others in my community." Her friend writes: "Emily is so happy that she has work that is emotionally and financially rewarding, fun, inspiring, and helpful to others in the community."

Now write a sentence in your journal about what you want to have happen in your life, and have your friend write your sentence in his or her journal. Agree to look at these sentences each day and visualize the events happening. When you do so, take a deep breath and feel, in your body, what the experience will be like when these goals have been accomplished. You and your friend might even write the sentences in your journals each day and look at them several times.

When you exchange mastermind visions with at least

one other person, you open yourself to the magic in the universe. You may find that, as you read your passionate sentence each day, it takes on more life. It may even change or become more specific. Rewrite your sentence as it changes, and let the vision keep growing in your mind and in your heart.

Put It in the Wind

Visioning and masterminding in the pages of your journal are powerful tools for manifesting what you want, but sometimes being attached to the results can get in the way. I've attempted to manifest a winning lottery ticket at my husband's request many times, to no avail. I'm not sure what creates that perfect formula for manifesting your dreams, but I believe it involves a combination of passion and detachment. There seems to be a fine balance between creating a passionate vision and surrendering that vision to the higher good. My wonderful friend Rick Wright, a therapist and life coach,[5] uses the phrase "put it in the wind" to describe this process. It means giving your vision a voice and setting it free into the universe. By speaking your beautiful, inspiring vision out loud and writing it in your journal, you tell the universe exactly what you want. Then you release it, trusting that if it's meant to be, it will be.

Often we very much want something to happen, but it doesn't — or it doesn't happen as quickly as we think it should. That is when our doubting inner critic sneaks back in. It's easy to doubt when you look around and things are not unfolding according to *your* plans and desires. You may be under financial stress or struggling with health issues. There are many situations that can drain your faith in the power of manifesting. These are the times to remain true to your vision. It's easy to throw your hands up to the sky and beg and plead with the heavens to grant your wishes. But the universe doesn't usually respond to desperation. You must find your inner peace. A state of calm, centered inner peace is essential to manifesting your dreams. When you are pushing too hard for your vision to unfold exactly the way you think it should, you could be pushing even more incredible opportunities and events away from yourself.

There is a place inside you that knows you will be okay, no matter how things turn out. That is the place from which to manifest your dreams. Keep your vision in front of you. Post it on your bathroom mirror, inside the front cover of your journal, and wherever you will be able to look at it often. When you are feeling beaten up or drained from rejection and confusion, read your vision again. Bring yourself back to the inspired moment when the words came pouring out of you and the path was crystal clear. This is the best place from which to live your life. This is where your life's purpose will appear.

Perhaps you have already mapped out your life's purpose; your plan is in place and you are pursuing your dreams. Even in that case, I urge you to remain open to other possibilities. The universe may have something even bigger in store for you. I once saw an inspiring conversation between Oprah Winfrey and author Iyanla Vanzant on television.[6] The two women were expressing their amazement at the generosity of

God's gifts. Earlier in her life, Iyanla had dreamed about who she wanted to be. Eventually, she discovered that no matter how big her dream was, God had an even bigger dream for her. In her book *One Day My Soul Just Opened Up* she writes, "None of what I am experiencing is what I asked for, and all of it is better than I would have ever dared to ask for."7

So when you create your visions in your journal, leave a little wiggle room for the incredible and possibly surprising gifts the universe can bring.

Try This
Put It in the Wind

Now it's your turn. In your journal, create a vision of that perfect wedding, birth, job, relationship, or whatever is on your mind. Start with just one area of your life, then move onto an entire life vision. Don't let anything hold you back. If David Cassidy can come to my house, then imagine the crazy and wonderful things you can create in your life! Let yourself go, and write from your heart. That is where your real dreams lie dormant. It's time to awaken them and give them some energy. Your vision should be something that moves you and inspires you to action. If you are creating financial abundance, go beyond just naming a dollar amount; write about what this abundance will feel like and how your daily life will be affected by it.

Infuse your vision with passion and write from your deepest desires. Think of the times when you have experienced real joy; what were you doing then? Write about those experiences and how you can create more of them. No dream is too big or too small to deserve attention. Release your desires and watch them unfold before your eyes.

Endless Possibilities

The possibilities for your life are endless; the universe is just waiting for you to ask. All you have to do is choose the life you want. Go in the direction of your dreams, stay connected to what feels right to you, keep your heart open, and watch for serendipity to work in your favor.

This excerpt from Max Ehrmann's poem "Desiderata" speaks to the heart of journaling:

> *You are a child of the Universe, no less than the trees and the stars; you have the right to be here. And whether or not it is clear to you, no doubt the universe is unfolding as it should. Therefore be at peace with God, whatever you conceive Him to be. And whatever your labors and aspirations, in the noisy confusion of life, keep peace in your Soul.*[8]

Your journal will help you keep peace in your soul. It will be your guide. It will open your heart and reveal your dreams. You only have to pick up a pen and begin writing.

If you still feel confused about what you want to do or be, chapter 7 will show you how to ask for help from your spiritual advisers — and how to hear their answers. From expanding your gratitude to receiving answers in your dreams, the resolution is always inside you; you only have to be still and listen.

CHAPTER 7

Conversations with Angels, Elvis, and Beyond

"If you build it, they will come," whispers the voice in the movie *Field of Dreams*. The farmer doesn't know where the whisper is coming from or exactly what it means. As the movie progresses, the whisper gets louder: "If you build it, they will come. Go the distance." When the farmer follows this voice — of God or intuition or whatever it is — magical things happen.

Have you ever heard a whisper like that? You've probably heard something crazy whispered in your mind's ear — and you immediately shrugged it off. "I can't do that! That's ridiculous!" What did the whisper say? Was it really such a crazy idea? It doesn't matter who is doing the whispering — God, Buddha, or Elvis — we need to pay attention when it happens.

We all have these whispers, but they often get drowned out by the other voices in our heads. You can increase your ability to hear the whispers of your soul by journaling. Honoring these whispers will connect you with your passion, purpose, and creativity. Many times, these whispers or intuitive thoughts are just glimpses of what is possible.

Do you look at people who have created an abundant life doing work they love as being unique, talented, and perhaps different from you? Using your journal as a tool, you can cultivate your whispers and your intuition; this will assist you in creating an abundant and passionate life of your own. You can follow your creative urges, map out infinite possibilities, and find that your guides or higher wisdom are on call for you twenty-four hours a day. All you have to do is ask. This chapter is about cultivating your inner creativity, communicating with a higher wisdom for answers to your deepest questions, and tapping into this unlimited source for guidance and inspiration.

We've talked about many ways to use your journal for healing and manifesting in your life. We've explored ways to dig deeper and cleanse past experiences and relationships. We've looked at using your journal to embrace change and help you navigate some of your big life lessons. We've also tried a few techniques and heard from people who have used their journals to manifest their deepest desires and create a life that they once only dreamed of. Now we come to another way to use your journal: to connect with a higher power, tap into your creativity, and hear your inner wisdom.

We will explore a journaling practice that includes finding your flow and cultivating your creative and spiritual connection. If you've ever wanted to express yourself creatively or use journaling as a spiritual practice, this chapter will get you started on the path.

Creativity

What is creativity? What makes a person creative? Some people refer to God as the Creator, and many artists believe that their art is divinely inspired — that it comes from a higher source. Artists in all media say that they connect to this source of inspiration when they enter a state of nothingness, or flow. An actor describes the feeling of letting go during a scene; he allows his instincts and emotions to overtake him, resulting in a performance that wins him an Academy Award. A musician composes a song during a moment of pure energy that lasts less than one hour; it becomes a number-one hit, touching millions of people. A writer talks of "taking dictation from another source" as her fingers type the words that will be translated into many languages and read by millions of people around the world.

In our culture, we tend to put artists on a pedestal. We worship their ability to express themselves in a way that inspires others. But are we really different from these artists? Do we so-called normal people have the ability to tap into this Divine inspiration and apply it in our own lives? The answer is a resounding "yes!" Journaling is one way to enter this state. I have seen ordinary people — accountants, contractors, social workers — search for a connection to something greater, and find that connection on the blank page. You can give yourself over to the magic of ink and paper, find your creative inspiration, and communicate with your inner wisdom or whatever spiritual source your upbringing and experience allows you to imagine. Then your journal will begin to reveal your hidden creativity.

In order to cultivate this creativity, you must give yourself a little time to just *be*. This can be challenging in our world of overstimulation. You must find a way to carve out real down time, which means allowing yourself to do absolutely nothing. In those moments of nothingness, your creativity emerges like bubbles rising to the surface. Relax and let your life flow like water, around you, over you, and through you. Taking your journal on these nothingness breaks ensures that you will capture the next creative inspiration.

Your journal is your direct ticket to *being*, or nothingness. It doesn't matter what may be swirling around you — you could be sitting in an airport or waiting in line for a driver's license — journaling has a way of quieting your mind. Jot down a few sentences about your outer world, then fall into yourself; observe your inner thoughts and musings and then write from the part of you that is always watching.

I love this journal entry from musician and author Jewel. To me, it sums up what it means to just be.

For two consecutive days I have been completely alone. How lovely it is to be alone. Today I am a normal, anonymous person who gets to sleep in. I get to sit in a café at the table by the window and watch people's lives unfold. I get to walk into the park and lie on my back and stare at the leaves and blue sky for hours and let my mind do what it was made to do: imagine and absorb and think and wander and suppose and speculate and watch. With no agenda. Just be.[1]

Writing in your journal makes you an artist, too. You are taking time to reflect and ponder life. You are stepping outside the parameters of your daily grind to notice your world. Part of *Webster's* definition of *artist* is "one who exhibits sensitivity." Journaling allows you to become more sensitive to your surroundings by asking you to slow down and capture the moment in your own unique way.

Try This
A Date with Nothingness

Take a short "nothingness break" with your journal. For ten minutes, drop whatever you are doing, stare out a window, rock in a rocking chair with your eyes closed, or lie down in the grass and try to move clouds. Take three deep breaths. Feel the breath go all the way down into your belly, then exhale any stress or tension you may be holding in your body. Imagine that your creativity is buried just beneath the surface of your skin. As you breathe in and out, the bubbles of creativity rise to the surface. Then write in your journal: "My creativity is expressed in..." and complete the thought. For a few minutes, write anything that pops into your mind. Are you going to write a novel or the lyrics of a song? Don't get hung up on defining creativity or thinking about how you're not creative; just list all the things in your life that you create. Your creativity could be in your garden or arranging furniture or baking. Write everything you already do that's creative and everything you'd like to do in the future that is creative in any way.

Now try drawing the first thing that catches your eye when you look up from your writing. Artistic expression is really just noticing the little things that most people miss, so examine the details around you.

Taking these few extra minutes to explore what's going on inside your heart and in the world around you encourages your creativity to come out and play. Try to make a nothingness date again in the next few days. Keep it up!

Gratitude

When you slow down long enough to notice the details around you, you will be awed by the beauty and abundance in the world. This is a good time to express your thankfulness for all that you have and all that you are going to create in your life. Keeping a gratitude journal is nothing more than writing down a few things each day that you are grateful for, yet this practice holds magical powers.

Here's a way to change your perspective faster than anything you've ever seen. Keep a journal on your nightstand.

Each night before nodding off, write the numbers one through five vertically on a page, then fill in the blanks with things you're grateful for. You will begin to look for things throughout your day to write down. This practice shifts your focus away from what is wrong in your life to what is right and beautiful and kind in the world.

Another way to do this is to keep a gratitude journal in the kitchen and jot down a few things from the day before as you sip your first cup of coffee in the morning. This is a lovely ritual for beginning your day on a positive note. I guarantee that if you set your alarm ten minutes early and do this, you will have a better day.

You can also carry a pocket journal around with you, small enough to fit into a purse, briefcase, or jacket pocket. As you go through the day, jot down inspirations and wonderful things as they happen: the children waving from the car next to you in traffic, the smell of freshly baked bread as you pass the bakery on the way to work, the newly paved expressway, the fact that your car started this morning, looking up from your work and discovering it's almost time to go home.

Once you get going, gratitude will overflow from your journal because there are always so many things to be grateful for. Therein lies the magic of expressing gratitude in your journal. It connects you to a state of appreciation that spills over into everything you do and experience. It inspires you to view your life from a state of grace, rather than a state of lack.

Nancy, a workshop participant and a mother of three, told me that she usually journals when she's angry or upset;

most of her journal entries "probably leave me looking like quite a mess, with out-of-control kids and a crappy husband." But Nancy's journal began to look different when she started writing down what she was grateful for:

> *I am sitting here tonight, and my babies are sleeping peacefully. The windows are open and the breeze is blowing the curtains, and I feel like the luckiest person alive. They are so precious, like little angels, truly. I yelled too much today. Poor Hannah, she's been such a little terror. I look at her sleeping, and all that other stuff just melts away. I am so blessed.*
>
> *So tonight here's what I am thankful for: my children sleeping sweetly while I have a moment to myself, cool winter nights and breezy curtains, my handyman husband, spaghetti dinners 'cause they're so easy, and my mom who made me laugh today with her goofy self.*

When you use gratitude in your journals, your heart will gradually open to the world around you. This will also help connect you with your creativity, and eventually with your intuition and inner wisdom.

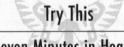

Try This

Seven Minutes in Heaven

Take the next seven minutes and write down at least seven things you feel grateful for. It will shift your mood immediately. Now see if you can keep this up for seven days. It doesn't matter when you do this — morning, noon, or night. Just try for seven days to gather seven things to write down. It's only seven days; if you miss a day, just keep going. Start right there in the moment when you notice something you're grateful for, and jot it down. Right that second! Don't beat yourself up for forgetting to write sooner; just move forward with your gratitude. You can write, "I'm so grateful I remembered to do this," and keep going with your day.

Some days it may feel like the only thing to be grateful for is that the day is over. That's okay, too. It won't be long before you notice the shifts — a slight feeling of lightness as you wake up, a bounce in your step, smiling at strangers. These are some of the little ways in which gratitude can seep into your day. There is no wrong way to do this. Just have fun, make it a game, and see what happens.

———————————

Here's a journal entry from my husband, made when I was nudging him to keep a gratitude journal on a regular basis:

1. *I am so grateful that Denver just won the Super Bowl.*

2. *I am so grateful that I'm about to sleep for eight hours.*

3. *I am so grateful that I have shelter from the elements.*

4. *I am so grateful that I am in good health and my family is in good health.*

5. *I am so grateful that Sandy stopped yapping about journaling.*

Intuition

How do you make the leap from cultivating your creativity and writing about things you are grateful for to actually feeling guided in your daily actions? The answer lies in your intuition. Many people who come to my workshops are completely out of touch with their intuition. They say things like "I don't have any intuition," or "I haven't had an intuitive thought in years." This just means that they're out of practice. Hearing the voice of your intuition requires stillness and awareness. It's always there, but it's one of those things that will get stronger and stronger as you give it your attention.

There are entire books written on the subject of developing your intuition. In his beautiful book *Spiritual Serendipity*, Richard Eyre suggests dividing your daily planner into two columns. Write your normal schedule and to-do list in the left column, and in the right column write any feelings or urges you have during the day. These can be anything: "had an urge to call Aunt Stella," "felt like I should follow up with Bob from New Star," "heard an ad for a new restaurant and wanted to go there." Whatever feelings or urges come up, write them down. Eyre defines *serendipity* as "a quality of mind which, through awareness, good fortune, and wisdom, allows one to frequently discover something good while seeking something else."[2] Reviewing the right-hand column of your list at the end of the week may surprise you, and following these urges could lead to some serendipitous results.

The next step in developing your intuition is learning to

trust your inner wisdom when it does show up. You are constantly being guided from within, but you may dismiss a brilliant idea or inclination because it feels weird or people might think you're crazy. Listen to the whispers, take the leap, and trust yourself. At the very least, trust yourself long enough to write it down. You can go back and discard it later if it doesn't make sense for you. Just get those thoughts and feelings down in black and white, and worry about the rest later. The crazy thoughts that you're judging now may be the first glimmer of your destiny. Before your lightbulb moments have a chance to shine, do you switch off the electricity and extinguish the power to ignite your dreams? The first step in connecting to a higher wisdom is surrendering to whatever shows up on the blank page.

Sometimes surrendering can seem difficult — especially if you are attached to a specific way in which you think things should unfold. You may tend to discount any other possibility or path. But there are usually many paths that lead to equally amazing results. The trick is to relax and let your inner wisdom guide you. Hold the vision of a wise, benevolent mentor smiling down on you, saying, "My child, there is no need to struggle. Relax. Everything is in Divine order."

I recently learned of a wonderful "cosmic insurance policy" that you can use if you have trouble surrendering to what may come. In her bestselling book *Creative Visualization*, Shakti Gawain suggests adding the following sentence to any goal or vision statement: "This, or something better, is now manifesting in totally satisfying and harmonious ways, for the highest good of all concerned."[3] Writing this or saying it to yourself as you tap into your whispers will give you confidence that everything will happen just as it is supposed to happen, even if it doesn't look exactly the way you've imagined.

Try This
I Know That I Know

Write this prompt at the top of a new page in your journal: "I know for sure that..." Then write for at least ten minutes. If you get stuck, you can keep your hand moving by writing, "I don't know..." and filling in the blanks. This prompt will help you tap into the wisdom that lives inside you. It will also help you get to the questions that are nagging at your insides and give you a place to start asking for guidance.

Ask and You Will Be Answered

Last year I was asked to give a journalution workshop for members of Gilda's Club, a national organization named for Gilda Radner, the talented and beloved *Saturday Night Live* comedienne who died from cancer in 1989. Gilda's Club was founded to provide meeting places where people living with cancer, along with their family and friends, can connect with others to build emotional and social support. I accepted immediately. However, as the date approached I became unsure of myself. I questioned what I could possibly have to share with someone who has cancer. My passion for

journaling was evident, but how did that translate into helping or inspiring someone who was dealing with cancer, or
someone who had lost a loved one to cancer?

As I drove to the workshop, I prayed for guidance. I
asked the Divine energy of the universe to be with me during my presentation and help me provide support and inspiration to the workshop participants. I prayed that I would
stay open to guidance and follow whatever wisdom might
come. I envisioned the evening going smoothly. But when I
arrived, there were only a handful of people in attendance.
The workshop tested my resolve on many levels. One woman
seemed to be falling asleep on the sofa! I forced myself to
continue, trying to appear enthusiastic and at ease, but inside
I was asking myself "What am I doing here?"

In the past, I have always presented a standard thirty-
minute workshop at new venues, including a couple of writing exercises. I was especially fond of closing with the prompt
"Things I Love" (see chapter 6). However, as I got ready to
give the final prompt during this workshop, I was suddenly
moved to pick the prompt "Conversation with Your Ninety-
Nine-Year-Old Self" (see chapter 2). I led the participants
through a visualization, then had them write for ten minutes,
asking questions of this older, wiser version of themselves.

In chapter 2, I told the story of Robert, a man in his mid-
forties who was new to journaling and who had battled cancer
and suffered several heart attacks. My encounter with Robert
was at Gilda's Club that night. Now you know the other piece
of that magical experience: the exercise that led Robert to a
life-changing revelation was unplanned. Something guided
me to choose a prompt that I had never used in a first-time

workshop before. I followed my intuition, and the prompt "Conversation with Your Ninety-Nine-Year-Old Self" led Robert to a transformation in only ten minutes.

I am certain that the prayer I said on my way to Gilda's Club that night is what created the space for Robert's revelation. I am also certain that a higher wisdom then guided me. The experience was a great blessing to me, and a confirmation that when you ask for help, it will be there. Now, whenever I return to speak at Gilda's Club, Robert is there to greet me with a big hug.

Try This
Moving On Up

Write about a time in your life when you felt particularly close to a higher power. If you are comfortable using the word "God," write about that. Otherwise, you may think of Mother Earth or the energy that unites every living thing in the universe or whatever works for you. Write about how that connection felt: Did you feel guided in a certain direction? How did you feel physically? Did you feel energy coursing through your body? Did you hear a voice or a whisper? What did it sound like? What was the experience like for you? Imagine that you are back in that moment right now. Feel it, breathe in the experience. Describe what was happening for you in as much detail as possible. Then see if you can re-create the experience right now in your journal.

Conversations with the Wisdom of the Universe

The more comfortable you become with asking questions, being still, and listening for answers, the more you will be able to tap into all the wisdom of the universe. This means that even the biggest questions or dilemmas you find yourself contemplating may be answered on the blank pages of your journal. Many people use their journal as a way to talk with God, Spirit, or the Divine energy of the universe, just like going to a church or a temple or meditating. Neale Donald Walsch wrote in his bestselling book *Conversations with God,* "I decided to write a letter to God. It was a spiteful, passionate letter. What had I done to deserve a life of such continuing struggle? Before I knew it, I had begun a conversation and I was not writing so much as taking dictation."[4]

Every one of us has the ability to connect with this energy. Writing in your journal is just another way to open the channel and let it flow through you. Let's experiment with some of these practices as you begin your own conversation with God or Buddha or your angels or whoever wants to show up in your journal. For those who have trouble accepting the thought of a direct conversation with God, angels, or Spirit, you can view this as a connection with your own inspiration, which can be just as Divine as any other.

The object is to let your inhibitions go. The movement of your hand takes over, and soon you're completely lost in the act of writing. You have no idea what you are writing about; you are just taking dictation from another source. In Mr. Walsch's book, God says, "I talk to everyone. All the time. The question is not to whom do I talk, but who listens?"[5]

Many avid journalers report having things show up in

their journals that they don't remember writing. They describe the pen flowing along the page as if their hand is being guided. If you'd like to have this kind of experience, ask the real questions you have in your heart and believe that the answers will come to you.

Try This
I Wonder

When you are feeling confused or overwhelmed with a situation, do you find yourself thinking "I don't know what to do"? Try writing for a few minutes with this prompt: "I don't know what to do about..." Then write "I wonder if I should..." Using the word "wonder" opens up the space to let the answer come through. Keep writing, changing the prompt phrase around as if the answer is going to show up any second. Write the first thing that comes into your mind, no matter how crazy it may seem. Write "Maybe I should..." and again write the first thing that pops into your head. Do this several times for ten minutes, and see what possible paths appear that weren't there before.

———————————

James, a man in his mid-thirties who came to one of my first workshops, told me about a practice he'd been using for years. He would write to himself as if Spirit were giving him advice about his life. He came to believe that Spirit could be channeled into his journal by simply asking a question and writing the first thing that popped into his head. This technique helped him through some of his roughest times as he grew from an adolescent outcast into a loving partner.

James told me about a crushing experience he had in elementary school, and how he later used his journal to get past it. In fifth grade, several boys cornered him during gym class and began taunting him, circling around and calling him "freak" and "homo." It was the first time he realized that he was different — and that everyone else knew it. As an adult, after many failed relationships with men and feeling that he would never be able to completely trust another human being, he used his journal to ask for guidance. Here is what James found himself writing:

> *You have relived that gym class experience over and over in your life. You have used it as a way to keep others at arm's length. The time has come to embrace that little boy who was hurt so deeply. He is beautiful and innocent; he is kind and gifted. Once you are able to love the little boy you once were, you will create the possibility for others to love the man you are today.*

This wonderful man came to realize how much he had hated the little boy who was taunted and teased. He tortured himself for years for not fitting in with the other kids at school. He saw every potential relationship as a possibility of getting hurt again. As he worked on embracing the awkward little boy he once was, he was able to attract a loving partner and finally allow himself to be vulnerable in a truly committed relationship.

When you begin to struggle with questions that seem much bigger than your capacity to answer, you may doubt anything that pops into your mind. Trust what comes to you. Just allow yourself to write it down, no matter how silly or outrageous it may seem. You have to move through whatever is there to get into the flow, and your critical mind may try to stop you. You are probably so used to hearing this critical voice that it feels like the only voice in your head. But, believe me, it is not. There is a voice that is completely connected to a higher energy and that has access to a wisdom that will guide you and answer any question you may have.

Try This
Dear Worldly Wisdom

Start a dialogue in your journal with your inner wisdom — or the Goddess or Buddha or Jesus — whoever you feel will help you the most with whatever difficult situation you're facing. Begin by just asking "What should I do?" Tell this higher being everything that's on your mind. Get your problems and concerns out on the page. Rant and rave and ask all the hard questions that are driving you mad. Get rid of them so that you can stop focusing on them. Then take a breath and listen. An answer will be there. Don't judge it, just write it. Feel that you are channeling a wise spirit who has enough experience and wisdom to guide you. Keep asking, and keep writing.

You should be getting really good at this by now. It may only take a few minutes of forced writing to let go. Your brain wants to hang on and control everything that comes through your hand. But keep going; there will come a moment, a blissful moment, when you let go and just write and write and write. You won't even know what you're writing; it might seem like complete nonsense, but it won't matter because it will feel so good. Give yourself fully to this practice, and you will see miracles.

After doing this exercise, go back and read what you've just written. You may have to decipher some fast, sloppy handwriting, but you might be amazed at some of the things you wrote. It may not sound like your normal voice. You might be surprised at just how wise you really are.

Communication from Beyond

Developing your intuition and being open to your own wisdom will provide valuable guidance in your life. It can even become a link to friends and relatives who have passed on. I have a close friend named Lori, whom I've known since we were kids. Lori's mother died when she was eleven years old. We didn't talk much about it as children, but she recently told me about something that has changed how she views her mother's death, as well as her own life.

The information surrounding Lori's mother's death was always elusive. Some relatives had insinuated that her mother committed suicide. As you can imagine, Lori carried many painful emotions into adulthood. She could never understand why her mother wouldn't stay around to take care of her. Lori also harbored a secret fear that someday she might snap, just as her mother had. Several years ago, Lori went to a therapist who told her to write letters to her mother. As Lori wrote the letters in her journal, she expressed the anger of an eleven-year-old girl being abandoned by her mother. The letters seemed to help Lori feel more at peace and connected with her mother.

One day, while away from home on business, Lori realized that she was only two blocks from her childhood home. She had an overwhelming urge to drive by her old house. It had been over ten years since she had seen it. As she sat in front of the house, memories came flooding back to her. She cried for the little girl who lost her mother, she cried for her children who would never know their grandmother, and she cried for her mother whose pain had apparently been too much to bear. After thirty minutes or so, Lori started the car and drove away.

As she reached the end of the street, Lori heard a voice in her head say, "Go back." She didn't know why, but she turned the car around and once again stopped in front of her old house. She took a deep breath, and seconds later a woman knocked on her car window and asked, "Can I help you?" Lori was startled, and quickly explained to the woman that she had lived in the house across the street when she was a little girl, and since she happened to be in town she wanted to take a look. The woman's eyes filled with emotion. "Lori? Could that be you?" The woman had been a dear friend of Lori's mother. They'd spent afternoons talking and weekends barbecuing together. But their relationship had changed after Lori's mother remarried; her behavior became erratic, and the neighbors suspected alcohol and drugs.

Then she said, "I can't believe he got away with killing your mother." When she saw the horrified look on Lori's face, the woman asked, "You didn't know?"

Lori talked with the neighbor for over two hours about the details surrounding her mother's death, the police reports, and the investigation into Lori's stepfather. The woman kept apologizing for revealing this awful information and causing Lori more pain, but in fact this new insight had the opposite effect on Lori; rather than causing pain, it helped her release it. Twenty-seven years of being angry at her mother for abandoning her — years of feeling worthless and not good enough to keep her mother around — vanished during that conversation. (Lori hasn't confronted her stepfather; she lost touch with him after her mother's death, and she's still processing this new information.)

After that day, Lori used her journal to write letters to her mother, even though her mother would never hold the letters and read them. This journaling helped her release the repressed sadness she carried, which opened up a space inside her for new energy. Lori is absolutely certain that it was her mother guiding her that day, urging her to go back long enough for her neighbor to return home and see Lori in her car. Lori has always felt her mother around her like an angel, but now she feels an even stronger connection with her, and the energy feels lighter and more joyful. Lori knows it was her willingness to write those painful letters to her mother in her journal that developed her ability to trust her intuition and follow the urge to see her old home. If she had ignored the voice that told her to turn the car around, she probably would have carried the fear and self-doubt forever. That one seemingly small decision has had a tremendous effect on her life.

Over and over in my workshops, people tell stories of being guided by a higher power in their journals. They relate stories of angels and loved ones who have passed on showing up on the pages to give them messages.

Try This

Talk with an Angel

Begin by writing a letter to someone who has passed on. Tell this person anything that's on your mind. If you're angry at the person for leaving, let the words spill onto the page. If you miss the person terribly, write down the things you miss most.

Then take a deep breath and begin a letter to yourself from this angel — your loved one who watches over you. Imagine that your angel is sitting on your right shoulder, whispering in your ear. Take dictation from your angel. Of course, your mind may jump in and try to ruin everything; it will shout that you are making this all up and you are just writing a letter to yourself. Just for a moment, allow yourself to feel the essence of your angel; let your imagination take over and see what happens. If tears come rolling down your cheeks, let them roll. Pretend that your angel is right there with you. By recognizing the energy of your angel, you allow it to become a larger part of your daily life. You may get feelings or urges from your angel, now and in the future. Take this process slowly and do only what feels comfortable for you. But just like Neale Donald Walsch's conversation with God, you can have a conversation with anyone or anything you choose. Try it.

My wish is that you will experience the joy of journaling in a way that confirms how wise and wonderful you are and that you are connected to the most powerful energy in the universe at all times. I want you to believe that you already have everything you need to accomplish all that you dream of. When you write in your journal, I want you to feel the rush of "I can't believe I just wrote that!" Journaling is the ultimate tool to take you wherever you want to go. Dream big — dream the biggest dreams you can imagine. Every single one of them is within reach. It only takes belief on your part and the willingness to go for it.

I hope you've caught a glimpse of some of the amazing possibilities for your life. Now, are you ready to do whatever it takes to get there? Does your everyday "life" keep interfering? The next chapter will help. It wraps up this journey by giving you some tips for using journaling to keep the faith and to stay on the road to creating the life you were meant to have.

CHAPTER 8

Being You

How do you figure out who you truly are? I believe the process starts in your journal. You get to decide how you want to live your life and who you want to be. I also believe that you can become anything you decide to be and achieve anything you want to accomplish. The following exercise will get you started on the path, then we'll go into more detail in the rest of the chapter.

Try This

Affirm How Wonderful You Are

Make a list of ten wonderful qualities you already possess, or ten qualities you would most like to cultivate. Tell yourself that it is safe to be *you* and that you already are all of these wonderful things.

If unwanted feelings come up in the process, write about them in your journal. Go back and revisit the earlier activities in this book: Name your emotions, complete your incompletions, and forgive; describe your perfect day, create a vision for what you really want, and begin to manifest your best life. Then continue affirming your inner beauty, grace, and power.

For example, here is an affirmation that a friend of mine created: "It is safe to be Jennifer. I am funky, intelligent, creative, wise, multifaceted, powerful, rich, exciting, joyful, energetic, healthy, and connected to Spirit. I bring that special Jenniferness to everything I do."

Creating a life you love is a process. A few days you will have quantum leaps, and other days you may feel like you're sliding backward. This is normal. This is life.

Life Happens

Okay, you've "found yourself." Now what? You had some moments of Divine inspiration, and the celestial energy of the universe spoke to you. Then the phone started ringing, the kids started fighting, and your boss told you that your deadline's been moved up three weeks. How can you use your journal to maintain your Divine momentum? How do you stay true to the vision you've created for yourself when life keeps interfering?

For most of my life, I've been waiting for something to happen. I would tell myself, "When such-and-such happens, then I'll be happy." When I have a million dollars, when I get married, when I figure out what I want to do with my life, when I get my book published — then I can really start living my life, then I will be happy, then my life will be perfect. The problem is that there's always something else to wait for or to accomplish.

No one's life is perfect. Many people look as if their life might be perfect on the outside, such as celebrities. Most celebrities are beloved and gorgeous, doing work they love, fantastically celebrated for doing this work, *and* getting paid astronomical amounts of money for it. Could life get any better than this? If we were rich and famous celebrities, then we'd be *really* happy, right? But celebrities also deal with a few things that are not so fabulous: paparazzi following their every move and cutting them off in traffic, people looking through the gates surrounding their homes as if they lived in a zoo, tabloids speculating about the intimate details of their lives. Do you think you might get agitated if you had to deal with this on a daily basis? You might flip out one day and have your picture splashed across the *National Enquirer*, attacking some newshound who was going through your garbage. My point is this: don't waste your energy wishing you were someone else; everyone's life has its delights and its challenges.

If you think about your life long enough, you will probably find lots of things that you really like about it. And that is the key: finding the things in your life that you *really* like and expanding them — feeling these moments as they are happening, capturing them in your journal, and celebrating them now.

Take a breath before you read this next sentence. It's even difficult for me to write. Are you ready? *You are never going to get there.* It's true. Wherever you are struggling to get, you are never going to arrive. Do you know why? Because there is no "there" to get to; you are there right now. Our lives are not and never will be stagnant. We are constantly in motion. When we try to hold on too tightly, life just slips through our fingers like water. It's easy to fantasize about a finish line and think that *then* our lives will be terrific. But it just doesn't work that way. And it's self-defeating to live that way. There will always be another imaginary finish line just out of reach. Our lives are made up of consecutive mountains and valleys, ups and downs. Sometimes we are climbing and struggling, and other times we are coasting, flying downhill. It's seductive to think in those moments of triumph that we've arrived; we are fabulous, we've figured it all out, and everything will fall into place perfectly from now on. Then life takes an unexpected turn, and we feel confused or betrayed: "Hey! I thought I was done with all of these life lessons. I thought I'd figured everything out. What happened?"

Life happened. You *are* fabulous. You *have* figured some

things out, but life will still happen because you are human. The journey of your life is just that: a journey. It is not a grand marathon that you must struggle through to reach the big finish, crowds cheering "You made it!" When you reach the finish line, you will be dead. Don't wait until then to begin enjoying your life. Don't wait until you can see the finish line before you take part in the celebration of it all.

Embrace this fact: as we live, we grow. If we are not growing, we are dying. Don't try to avoid it, welcome it. Love it. Revel in it. Sometimes weeds show up, but weeds are really hidden opportunities to make your garden even more wonderful. They call you to pay attention, notice the wonderful little details, and put some energy into it all.

Finding yourself — your passion and purpose — is just one step on this incredible journey of life. It's not always easy, but it is always extremely rewarding. Some people figure it out early, and others spend a good portion of their lives finding themselves. *Staying* yourself is the true essence of life.

Once you have created a vision for your life, your journal will keep you on track. It will be there to remind you of your greatness. We all have the possibility for greatness. I firmly believe that each of us comes into this world to contribute something — our unique voice. Part of life is figuring out what that voice stands for, who you are, and what your contribution will be. Your journal will help you do this. It will also help you make a plan to express your voice in the world. Your journal will continue to be there as you put the plan into action, urging and nudging you along the path.

Your journal will maintain your vision. It will keep you in touch with your inner wisdom when you feel you've gone off track or gotten lost. Your journal will guard the focal point for your vision. Every time you feel lost or overwhelmed, it will be there, keeping you in touch with the wiser parts of yourself.

Here's a journaling exercise that will help you create a sentence that evokes joy. This sentence will keep you on track with your life's vision and in touch with your inner wisdom.

Try This
Finding Joy

Take a deep breath and remember yourself as a child. What were some of your most joyful childhood moments? Write them down. Now move through your growing years and write about more joyful moments in grade school, high school, and college. Now think about your adult life. What have been some of the most joyful experiences in adulthood for you? When was the last time you felt real joy — laughter bubbling up from within, a stillness or feeling of contentment? Write about this.

As you think about these joyful moments, is there a common theme? What types of things have brought you the most joy? See if you can boil these thoughts down to one statement that sums up the theme of your joy. Create a sentence to call more of these joyful moments into your life. Put it somewhere to make you smile. Go find your joy!

A great example of incorporating joy into your life comes from comedienne Elvira Kurt. In an interview, she mentioned that her family often criticized her as a child, saying, "You think everything is so funny," in the way only one's family can.[1] Undaunted, Elvira fashioned her humorous take on life into a career in comedy. Now it's her job to look at life and find the funny moments. She could have listened to the critical voices around her and grown up to get a "real" job, stifling her innate ability to find humor in life. Instead, now she shares her funny thoughts with the world — and gets applause for doing so.

Here is a journal entry sent to me by a young woman in California:

> *I find that when I look in the mirror lately, instead of looking at a stranger, I feel love. I see someone pretty and warm and kind. I like her. I smile at her. It's a nice feeling. I like it. I will focus on helping that feeling grow.*

Playing Small or Living Large

I once spoke at a women's conference at the local convention center. The organizers were expecting five thousand to ten thousand people, but the actual attendance was much lower. The venue was huge, the stage large. A speaker was on stage when I arrived, and two people were sitting in the seats in front of the stage; a few more were milling around the booths nearby. As I got closer, I heard the speaker say to the sound man, "Should I just stop? I'm not exactly capturing anyone's attention." My heart sank for her and fear rose up in my belly. I'd been speaking, giving workshops and presentations, for many years. I'd spoken at conferences in front of hundreds of people, and I'd spoken at bookstores when only one person showed up. In the latter case, we would sit in chairs and just share our stories with each other. But this was different. This was *supposed* to be a big crowd. There was a stage. There was no possibility of sitting in chairs and relating one-to-one. I would have to stand on that stage, alone with a microphone, and succeed or fail. I could feel my heart pounding and my stomach sinking. I knew all too well how the woman on the stage felt. She felt like throwing the microphone down and running away.

The statistics about fears of public speaking popped into my head. Public speaking is ranked as the number-one fear, before death. Jerry Seinfeld jokes that this means most people attending a funeral would rather be the guy in the coffin than the guy giving the eulogy.

I went to the bathroom to gather my thoughts. I knew I had it in me to run away. I have played small for much of my life; it is a comfortable role for me. But I also knew that a larger part of me knew exactly what to do. I remembered the vision I had been journaling about for years. I imagined the greatest speakers of our time; what would they do? Of course, they would get up there and share their message, undaunted by the lack of enthusiasm in the crowd. They would generate their own enthusiasm. There in the bathroom, I talked to myself: "Damn it, Sandy! You can do this. *Be* who you really want to be, now!"

I walked onto the stage and envisioned hundreds of people cheering and excited about my talk. I imagined that I was practicing for the next time I would be in front of a large audience. I forced myself to have fun with it. I projected my energy as far as my eyes could see, and I connected with as many people as I could. I pretended that I was the most practiced, uplifting speaker in the world. I did my best. For that, I am so grateful. I wanted to run away. It would have been easier to acknowledge the poor turnout and take everything in my presentation down one notch. The feedback from the event sponsor was very good, but more important was how I felt when it was over. A glow seemed to be coming from the center of my body. For that moment, I knew for sure that I was in the perfect place, doing exactly what I was meant to do with my life.

This is a feeling I have been searching for my entire life. Those moments are becoming more and more common these days, as I move closer to the vision I created in a journal many years ago. There are good days and bad days. My journal reflects much of both. It is my life, living and breathing on the pages of my journal. Keeping a journal forces me to remember my dreams and reminds me to live up to them when the opportunities present themselves. Journaling is a way for you to stay connected to your goals and visions when life happens. Journaling will bring you back to that place where the dreams first whispered to you. It will keep you excited and believing that everything is possible.

A few more journaling prompts to keep you in touch with who you want to be in your life follow.

Try This
Personal Ad

Set a timer for ten minutes and write "Personal Ad" at the top of a blank sheet of paper. Now, for ten minutes, describe yourself. Don't worry if you are already married; this is just for fun and creativity. Who are you? How do you look to others? What are the most striking qualities of your personality? Why would someone be lucky to spend the rest of his or her life with you? What makes you unique? Who are you, really? Don't worry about the facts; you can be completely philosophical or just describe your physical qualities. Let your mind wander and your pen lead the way. Have fun!

———————————

Here is a personal ad written by a recent journalution workshop participant:

I'm a petite 5'-3", with long, straight, light-brown hair and blue eyes, and a smile I'm told lights up a room. I'm smart, fun, and sexy. I play guitar, write songs, and sing. I am unique and I look at the world through an artist's eyes, talking to the animals, dreaming of rocking Madison Square Garden and sailing away into the sunset. I'm a walking contradiction, practical and sentimental, bold and shy, harsh and sensitive, a socialite with hermit tendencies. I love to read. I love to write. I love a good intellectual debate, but hate arguments. I want to be a channel of love and light in the universe and leave this world a better place by the actions in my life. I'm a revolutionary and I will fight for what is right, break rules that I don't believe in, and swim upstream in the face of blind conformity and nonconscious thinkers. I'm an Aquarius. I want to find a partner — a friend to share my life with, maybe make some babies, maybe not, maybe have adventures around the world, or find a beautiful place with a river or an ocean where we can make a home . . . after I rock Madison Square Garden.

Try This
Winning Lottery Ticket

Imagine that you have just won the lottery. Eighty million dollars is on its way to your bank account right now. Write about the first few months after the money arrives: quitting your job, traveling, giving lavish gifts, buying new homes and cars, meeting with financial advisors, setting up trusts and investments. Imagine that you've had the time of your life, and now you must figure out what to do with the next twenty or thirty years. What moves you into action? What makes you feel passionate about life? Who do you want to help? You still have time to lie on a deserted beach and drink frozen fruity concoctions, but that's sure to get boring after a year or two. What then? Take ten minutes and let your mind wander to the deepest, darkest corners. Instead of asking, "What do I want to do?" try asking "How can I contribute?"

Try This
Panel of Guides

Visualize a panel of superstar guides for your life. These people can be alive or dead. They can be famous authors, movie stars, or religious figures. Develop your dream team of guides to counsel you in every decision you make. This panel of experts will be sitting on your shoulder, ready and waiting to be called into action. The more you consult with them, the more active they become. Would you like Socrates, Buddha, or even Elvis to guide your career or relationship decisions? Write about why you want each person on your panel and the kinds of things you would consult each one about. What do you think each panel member would say about the state of your life right now? Use this panel to assist in making the big decisions in your life, or in simply deciding how to spend your day off. Have fun with your dream team of wisdom!

Other people may share their journeys and experiences with you, and some of these methods will be of great help and inspiration. But remember that, no matter what advice is out there, you will always be the best expert on your life. There is no better counsel to enlist in solving your problems or designing the life of your dreams than your journal and your inner wisdom. Call on your panel of guides, and trust that your answers will appear. It's all inside of you; you already have everything you need.

I heard a wonderful metaphor for taking responsibility for your own awakening. There are many teachers who can point you in the right direction, but that is all that they can do. A teacher can point to the moon, but that is where the teacher's guidance ends and the student's journey begins. Your teacher cannot pluck the moon from the sky and place it in your hands; you must follow the guidance and continue on your own, out into the darkness. Only then will you find the moon.

Choose

It's easy to believe all of your critical voices and never attempt anything risky or scary in your life. It's easy to play small. It's easy to abandon your dreams when you hear "Who do you think you are?" It takes more effort to step beyond your comfort zone and attempt to fulfill the whispers of greatness. I believe that those whispers are glimpses of what is possible. They are your soul or your inner wisdom or the universe showing you what can be, if you really want it. You always have a choice. This is your life. You must choose the life you want. And even if you decide not to choose, you are actually making a choice.

Your entire life is made up of choices — to react or not, to make a stand or shrink back, to follow a path or be still. These everyday choices add up to your life. Sometimes something big crashes in and causes your life to take a different turn; other times it feels like life is just rolling by on schedule, nothing important happening. Here is the lesson

I've learned from journaling: the everyday things, the seemingly mundane and ordinary, are the moments that make up your life. You can ignore them, or you can appreciate and celebrate them. Your journal is the perfect place to begin celebrating every moment of your life.

When I began my journal, I barely knew who I was. I wanted to heal from being abandoned by my father. I wanted to find a passion and purpose for my life — something that would fulfill me. I wanted to contribute to something larger than myself. Finally, I wanted to pass something along to my family — my children and my children's children. I heard a whisper of a possibility.

Slowly, magically, my life unfolded with dreams and desires beyond my wildest imagination. If the twenty-one-year-old girl who poured her heart out in that first black-and-white composition book — looking for some deeper meaning in her life — could see me today, she would hardly believe what she sees.

I hope this book and the journaling prompts inspire you to uncover your deepest dreams and desires. I hope you will trust your intuition and allow your higher wisdom to lead you to all the wonderful things you deserve. I know for sure that every one of us has an inner wisdom that is available to guide us. I know for sure that the glimpses we catch out of the corners of our busy lives are put there for a reason, and that anything we glimpse we can achieve, if we truly desire it. And I know for sure that a journal and a pen are some of the best tools for creating a map for the life of your dreams and calling out to the universe to bring all of those dreams to life.

It's up to you to give your life meaning and purpose. You can use up your moments worrying and wondering "what if?" or you can strike out on your own to find your answers. My wish is that you will use your journal to discover your passion, give back to the world, and celebrate your life.

You should never feel alone, never give up on your dreams, and never abandon hope that you have the answers. The answers are all there, possibly buried by worries or lists of things to do, but they can be excavated within your journal. As you pay closer attention, the whispers will get louder. All you have to do is ask, be still, and listen for the answers. Oh yeah, and then write them down in your journal.

Index of Journaling Exercises

Chapter 1: Where Do I Start?

Begin Where You Are   page 14
Interview with Yourself   page 16
Why Do I Want to Journal?   page 18

Chapter 2: The Digging Begins

I Remember   page 30
You...Only Younger   page 32

I Don't Want to Write About...   page 36
Conversation with Your
     Ninety-Nine-Year-Old Self   page 38
Taking Stock   page 41

Chapter 3: Cleansing and Celebrating the Past

Naming Your Emotions   page 46
Letter   page 50
Look Closely at Your Buttons   page 52
Completing Your Incompletions   page 53
Heal and Celebrate   page 56
Forgiveness   page 62
Ask a Question   page 63

Chapter 4: Expectations and Major Life Transitions

CEO: Chief of Emotions Officer   page 71
Dialoguing   page 74
Inspiration for Your Journal   page 76
You as the Hero   page 78
How Do I Love Thee?   page 81
Who Am I Now?   page 83
The Other Side of the Mountain   page 88

Chapter 5: Mirror, Mirror on the Wall

Mirror, Mirror on the Wall   page 99
What's Your Big Picture?   page 105
Reflecting and Connecting   page 107
Conversation with Your
     Inner Dreamer   page 110
Spread the Love   page 112
Meet the Masters   page 113

Chapter 6: Hopes, Dreams, and Visions

Things I Love   page 119
Is This What You Really Want?   page 120
Perfect Day   page 125
The Manifesting Game   page 128
The Dinner Party   page 130
Mastermind   page 133
Put It in the Wind   page 136

Chapter 7: Conversations with Angels, Elvis, and Beyond

A Date with Nothingness   page 143
Seven Minutes in Heaven   page 146

I Know That I Know   page 150
Moving On Up   page 152
I Wonder   page 154
Dear Worldly Wisdom   page 156
Talk with an Angel   page 160

Chapter 8: Being You

Affirm How Wonderful You Are   page 164
Finding Joy   page 168
Personal Ad   page 172
Winning Lottery Ticket   page 173
Panel of Guides   page 174

Journalution Group Guidelines

Getting Started

When two or more gather together, miracles happen! If you want to start a journalution group, you don't need to wait until you have several other members to get started — even two people can experience magical energy when sharing the journaling prompts. You only need one other person, and you're ready to go. Set up a time to meet so that you can review these guidelines, and begin journaling!

Helpful Hints

These suggestions will help you create a safe space for a successful and productive group meeting. They will keep your meetings running smoothly and assist in preventing situations that can cause discomfort among your members. We suggest that you begin each meeting by reviewing the following agreements:

1. Confidentiality

    Everyone should make a commitment to confidentiality. This is of utmost importance to maintaining trust within the group. The topics of the journalution group meeting and any private information that is shared are to be kept strictly confidential.

2. Use a timer

    A timer makes it easy to do the timed journaling exercises, and it allows the facilitator to let go of clock-watching and participate fully in each exercise. The timer should also be used when members are speaking. This ensures that each person has an equal opportunity to discuss what's on his or her mind. It also helps avoid having one member habitually dominate the conversation. An inexpensive timer that beeps — sold at grocery and drug stores — is extremely effective.

3.   Advice and criticism

Discourage unsolicited advice and criticism. Encourage members to speak from personal experience, and to say "I" rather than "you." Members will ask for any feedback they need on a particular subject. Focus on solutions rather than problems. Members may need to vent, but attempt to keep whining and complaining to a minimum and turn the attention to the role journaling can play in revealing a new path or solution. If one member seems to have trouble finding answers to a problem, encourage that person to seek professional guidance in addition to the journalution group.

4.   Facilitators

It's a great idea to rotate the position of facilitator within the group. At the end of each meeting, choose who will facilitate the next meeting. That person can be responsible for gathering any needed supplies and for planning an opening topic. The facilitator will also be in charge of setting the timer and keeping exercises and discussion flowing smoothly during the meeting. Rotating facilitators ensures that each member has an opportunity to give and receive support, and it prevents one person from having to take the role of boss or caretaker.

Meeting Format Suggestions

1. Begin each meeting by reviewing the group
    guidelines and allotting time for journaling
    exercises (e.g., five ten-minute timed writings)
    and for sharing (e.g., one to three minutes per
    member per topic).

2. Use the Index of Journaling Exercises on page
    179 to randomly select exercises, or have each
    member write a prompt on a slip of paper,
    then fold and toss it into a bowl or hat.
    Encourage members to collect new prompts to
    share with the group. Prompts can be anything:
    lines from books and poems, billboards,
    magazine ads, or phrases overheard on a bus.

3. Have one member draw a prompt and read it
    aloud to the group. The facilitator sets the
    timer, and everyone writes for the agreed
    amount of time. (Just keep those pens moving.)

4. Do one to three timed writings, depending on
    the group's decision.

5. Read your journal entries round-robin style,
    beginning with the person to the left of the
    member who drew the prompt, and continuing
    clockwise. If you've done more than one
    writing session, each member can choose which
    one to read. A member may *always* elect to pass.
    (You may also choose to refrain from sharing

until all the writings have been completed.
Sometimes just writing and then reading aloud
without comments can be liberating.)

6. Continue drawing prompts, doing timed
   writings, and sharing journal entries.

7. Close the meeting by asking if anyone has any
   other special journal entries, quotes, or poems
   they'd like to share with the group.

8. Agree upon the facilitator for the next meeting,
   and confirm the date and time of the next
   gathering.

Attracting New Members to Your Group

1. Send invitations

   Send invitations to friends and acquain-
   tances (you can check out a sample invitation
   at www.journalution.com). Arrange for an
   informal gathering to discuss the kind of
   journalution group you'd like to start and to
   share information about how the group would
   work. Invite everyone you think might have an
   interest in self-improvement, writing, spirituality,
   or getting in touch with their inner creativity.

2. You tell two friends, and so on and so on...

   When you send out invitations, ask people
   to bring along one or two friends. Then, each

time you meet, remind the members that they can bring a friend to the next gathering. Your group will grow quickly this way. Four to ten members is ideal. If you gather more than ten, you can break into smaller groups and then come back together at the end of the meeting — or have a larger gathering every month or two to share ideas and inspiration.

3. Post flyers around town.

    Use our sample flyer (www.journalution.com), or create one of your own. Be sure to include tabs at the bottom with your contact information so that interested people leave with your number and not the entire flyer. Leave your flyer where people gather: coffee shops, bookstores, health food stores, religious buildings, community centers, colleges, health clubs, grocery stores, salons, yoga centers, children's schools, and care centers.

Acknowledgments

This is my first book, and it feels as if I have been writing it my entire life; therefore, I really need to thank every person I have ever met. Thank you so much for your encouragements and your criticisms. I deeply value every lesson I've learned and every laugh we've shared.

I am enormously grateful to New World Library and Georgia Hughes for taking a chance on me; to Kristen Cashman and Carol Venolia for somehow channeling exactly what I meant to say; to Mary Ann Casler, Tona Pearce Myers, Marjorie Conte, and the rest of the incredible family at New

World Library, thank you, thank you, thank you. To my agent, Joe Durepos, thank you for your patient guidance and wonderfully detailed explanations and especially for holding my hand through this process.

To all the wonderful souls who have hosted Journalution workshops over the years, thank you for supporting me: David Cronin, Richelle Doliner, RSI Ft. Lauderdale, Cristina Nosti and Books & Books, Gilda's Club, GAP Girls and Junior League Miami; and thank you to Students Rock, for taking the Journalution on the road with you!

Thanks also to Marcelene Dyer for telling me I have my own book to write and continually guiding me in absolutely everything. Just being around you inspires me to be a better person. To Stephanie Gunning for "getting it" right away and then helping me find my voice through the proposal and first drafts. You've made me a better writer, and I thank you. To Rick Wright for being my angel, rescuing me from my breakdowns, and always revealing the next step. To Heide Banks for showing me my true "Sandy-ness." To Arielle Ford for providing invaluable insight and clear advice and for answering every question. To Julie, Diana, and Michelle of Smack the Bird Writing Group, and to Laura, Elaine, and Rochelle of M2M Mastermind Group for believing in me always. To Linda Sivertsen for getting me off my butt and moving in the right direction. To Kelly Churchill at Creative Cursor for designing and creating my website and every other amazing idea you've implemented in record time. You rock!

Thank you to John Offerdahl's incredible staff for feeding me healthy food during my writing marathons and giving me a lovely office away from home. To VSY, Happyland, Ms. Navarro, Barbara, Sierra, Artie, and Paulette for giving me the peace of mind that my little girls were always well taken care of.

I am eternally grateful to the many friends, Journalution workshop participants, and members of the online journaling groups who so generously offered their personal journal entries for this project. Thank you to everyone who read the early drafts of the manuscript and gave me invaluable feedback.

To my family and friends, thank you for always giving me a warm place to share the joy. Mom, Tony, Wendy, Keith, Heather, Paulette, Artie, and Andy, you all make my life really great. Haley and Emily, may your strength and beauty always shine as brightly as they do today. Rich, thank you for supporting me on this journey in every way, for serenading me with your beautiful songs, and for being my forever partner on this path we call life. I love you — so much.

Notes

Chapter 1: Where Do I Start?

1. David McCullough, *John Adams* (New York: Touchstone, 2001), 66.
2. From Oprah Winfrey's website (http: www.oprah.com).
3. Louise Hay, from an endorsement quote of the cover of Neil E. Neimark, MD, *The Handbook of Journaling* (Irvine, Calif.: R.E.B. Technologies, 2000).
4. Charles Dickens, *A Tale of Two Cities* (New York: Random House, 1996), 1.

5. Natalie Goldberg, *Wild Mind: Living the Writer's Life* (New York: Bantam Books, 1990), 4.

Chapter 2: The Digging Begins

1. Henry David Thoreau, *Walden* (New York: Random House, 1992).

Chapter 4: Expectations and Major Life Transitions

1. Sabrina Ward Harrison, *Spilling Open* (New York: Villard Books, 2000).
2. Dan Baker, PhD, *What Happy People Know* (New York: St. Martin's Griffin, 2004), 159.

Chapter 5: Mirror, Mirror on the Wall

1. Rachel Simon, *Riding the Bus with My Sister* (New York: Plume, 2003), 39.
2. The Dalai Lama, *The Art of Happiness* (New York: Riverhead Books, 1998).

Chapter 6: Hopes, Dreams, and Visions

1. Oprah Winfrey, "Passion: Interview with Salma Hayek," *O Magazine*, September 2003, 220.

2. Wayne Dyer, public lecture, Whole Life Expo, April 2000.

3. Napoleon Hill, *Think and Grow Rich* (New York: Ballantine Books, 1927, 1983), 148.

4. Laura Duksta, *I Love You More* (Hialeah, Fla.: I Shine, Inc., 2001).

5. Rick Wright, Wright Consultancy, Los Angeles, Calif., (http://www.wrightconsultancy.com).

6. Iyanla Vanzant in conversation with Oprah Winfrey, *The Oprah Winfrey Show*, April 1999.

7. Iyanla Vanzant, *One Day My Soul Just Opened Up* (New York: Fireside, 1998), 300.

8. Max Ehrmann, "Desiderata," *The Desiderata of Happiness: A Collection of Philosophical Poems* (New York: Crown, 1995), 10.

Chapter 7: Conversations with Angels, Elvis, and Beyond

1. Jewel Kilcher, *Chasing Down the Dawn* (New York: HarperCollins, 2000), 86.

2. Richard Eyre, *Spiritual Serendipity: Cultivating and Celebrating the Art of the Unexpected* (New York: Simon & Schuster, 1997), 5.

3. Shakti Gawain, *Creative Visualization: Use the Power of Your Imagination to Create What You Want in Your Life*, 25th Anniversary Edition (Novato, Calif.: New World Library, 2002), 28.

4. Neale Donald Walsch, *Conversations with God: An Uncommon Dialogue* (New York: Putnam, 1995), 12.
5. Ibid, 3.

Chapter 8: Being You

1. Elvira Kurt, interview by Diane Rehm, *The Diane Rehm Show*, National Public Radio.

Share Your Journal
with Us

I would love to hear about your experiences with the
material in this book. Please let me know what your
favorite stories and journaling exercises were and how they
affected you.

I also invite you to send me any of your journal entries
that had special meaning for you and that you'd like to see
published in future editions of *Journalution*.

For guidelines on how to submit your journal entries,
visit my website at www.Journalution.com.

You can also mail submissions to:
Journalution
1007 North Federal Highway, Suite 197
Fort Lauderdale, FL 33304

About the Author

S andy Grason regularly leads Journalution workshops and lectures on the topic of journaling for emotional healing, inspiration, self-expression, and manifesting, and as memoir. Her websites have become popular connecting points for avid journaling enthusiasts to share journal entries, use Sandy's techniques for inspiration, and to connect with other journalers to form local groups.

Sandy has been an avid journaler for more than fifteen years, and her mission is to inspire millions of people to use journaling to discover their hidden passions and inner wisdom. She lives in south Florida with her husband and two daughters.

www.SandyGrason.com
and
www.Journalution.com